The Colouring Collective presents

The Enchantment of Elves

By Kelly Horton

Copyright 2017 Kelly Horton

ALL RIGHTS RESERVED

With the exception of those used in review's, the uncoloured or blank images herein, may not be reproduced, in whole or part by any means exsisting, other than for review.

The pages contained within are for personal use only. You may not distribute to or share uncoloured blank pages with any other colourists, in colouring groups, colouring group parties, via Email or message etc to any other person, group, people or entity, and you may not upload blank or uncoloured pages to the internet without prior written permission of the artist and author Kelly Horton / The colouring Collective puplications.

For any further details, including information on other books or colouring pages contact:

Kellyartistthorton@yahoo.com

For more colouring pages:

www.etsy.com/uk/Colourcollectiveshop

For Video Tutorial search youtube:

The Colour Collective

~Dedication~

Firstly, a Thankyou to my supportive Family, My husband and our five children, who are always encouraging, supportive, and are always there to help and advise creatively.

Secondly, a special Thakyou to my Colouring team, whom have been colouring my pages, and providing feedback throughout the process of creating this book. I thank you for your hard work, your enthusiasm and your loyalty.

And finally Thankyou to you, the colourist. Without your passion for colouring I could not create these books. The colouring community has welcomed me with open arms, and in return, I hope to create books that continue to give you enjoyment.

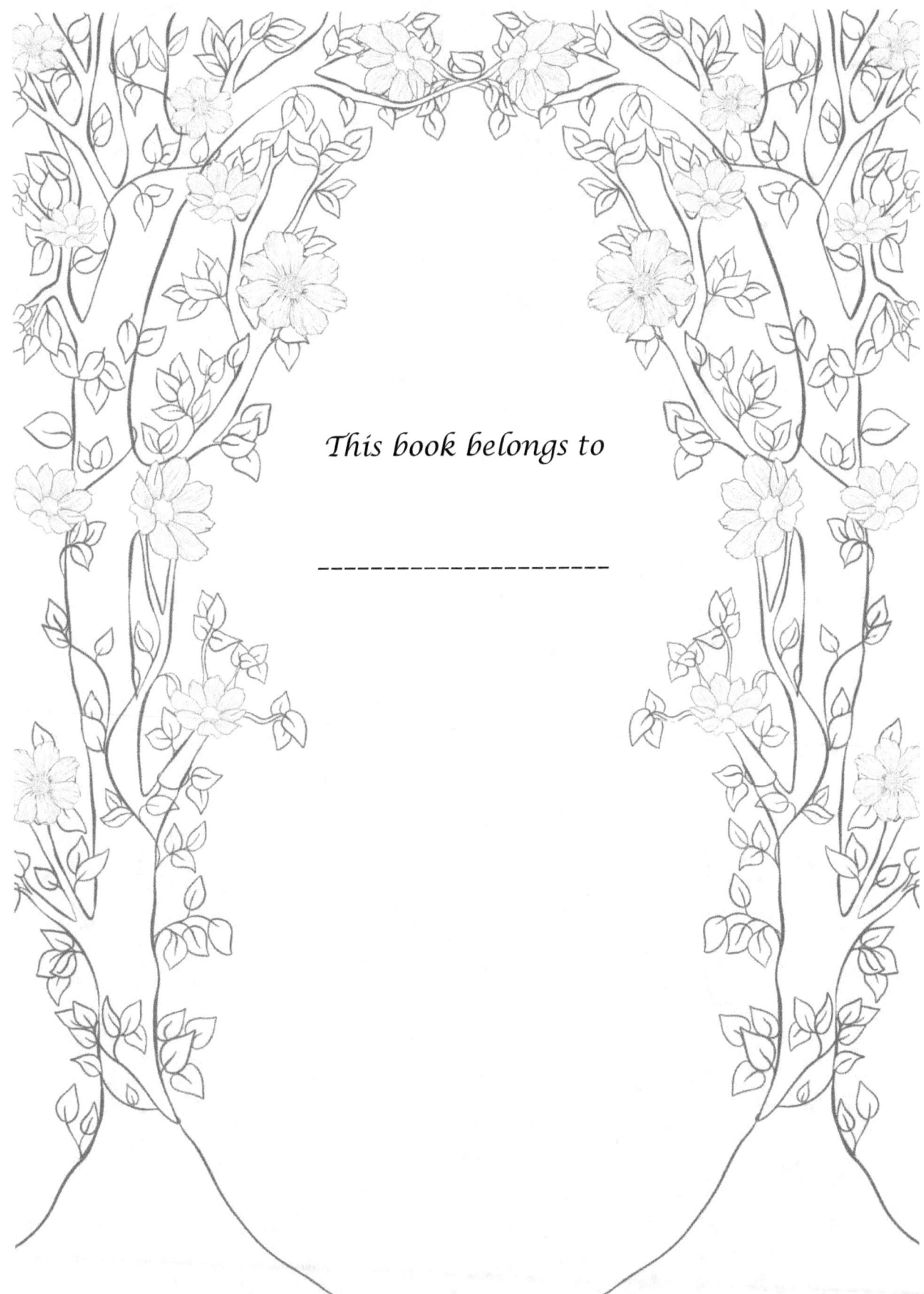

This book belongs to

_ _ _ _ _ _ _ _ _ _ _ _ _ _ _ _ _ _ _ _

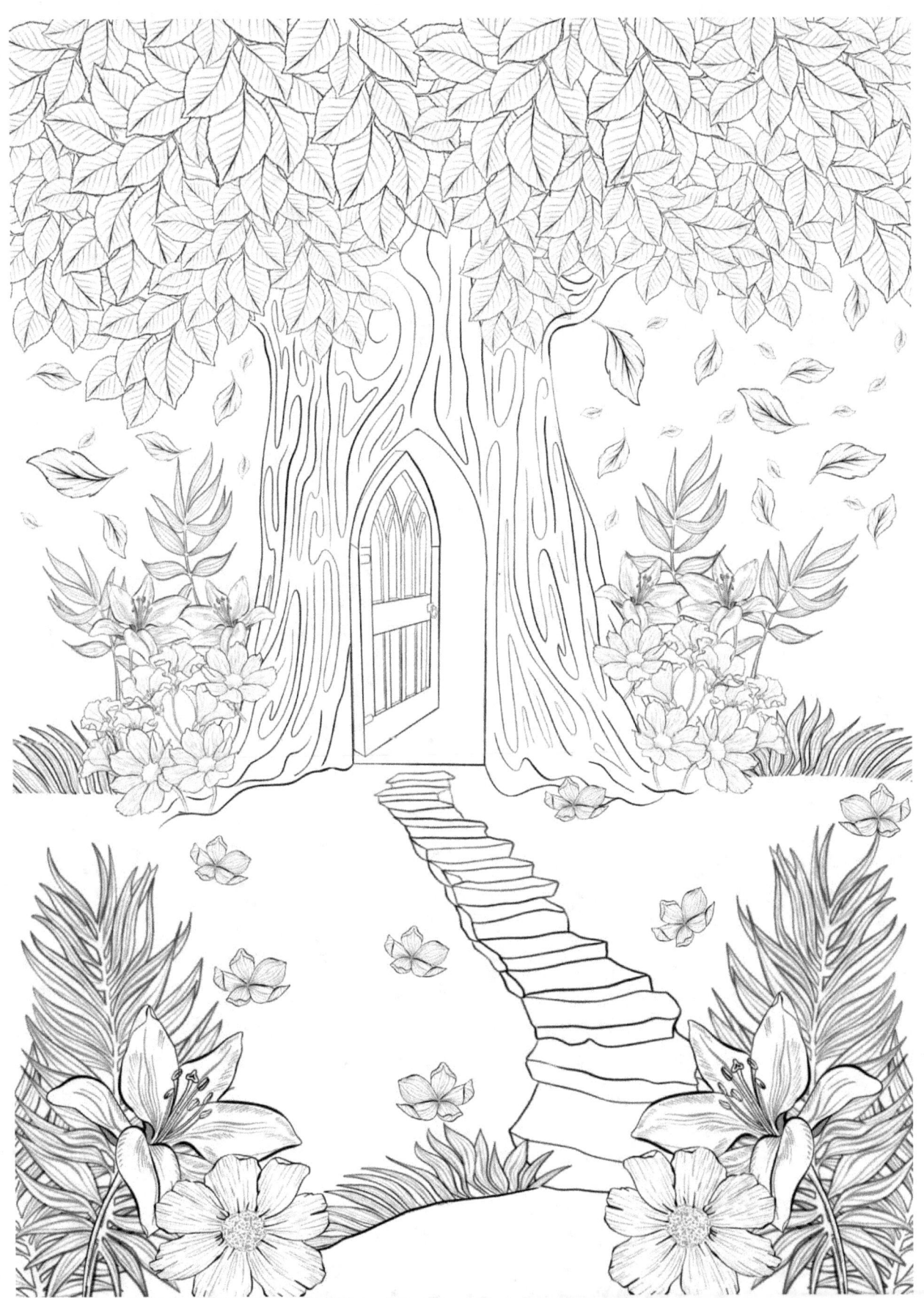

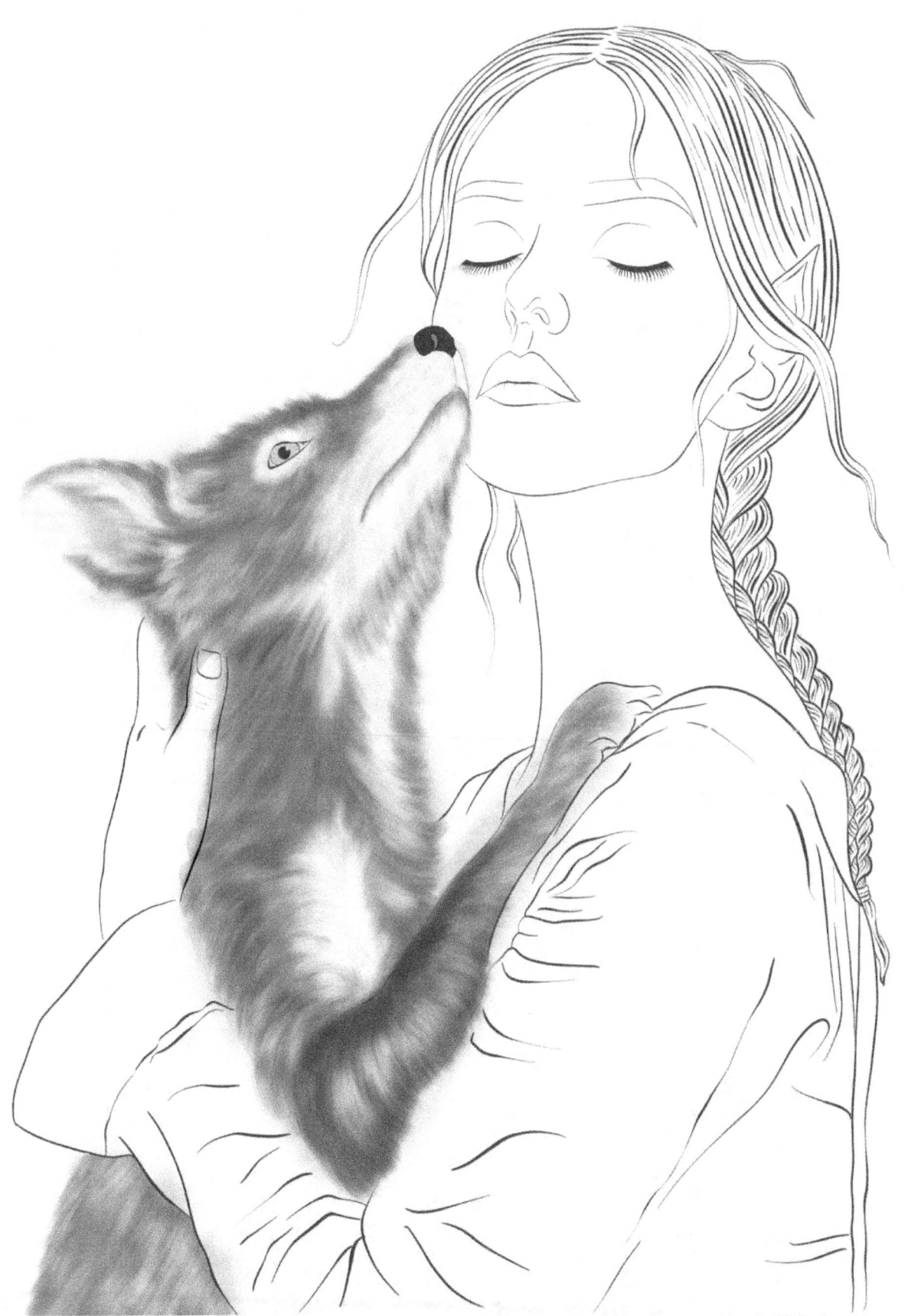

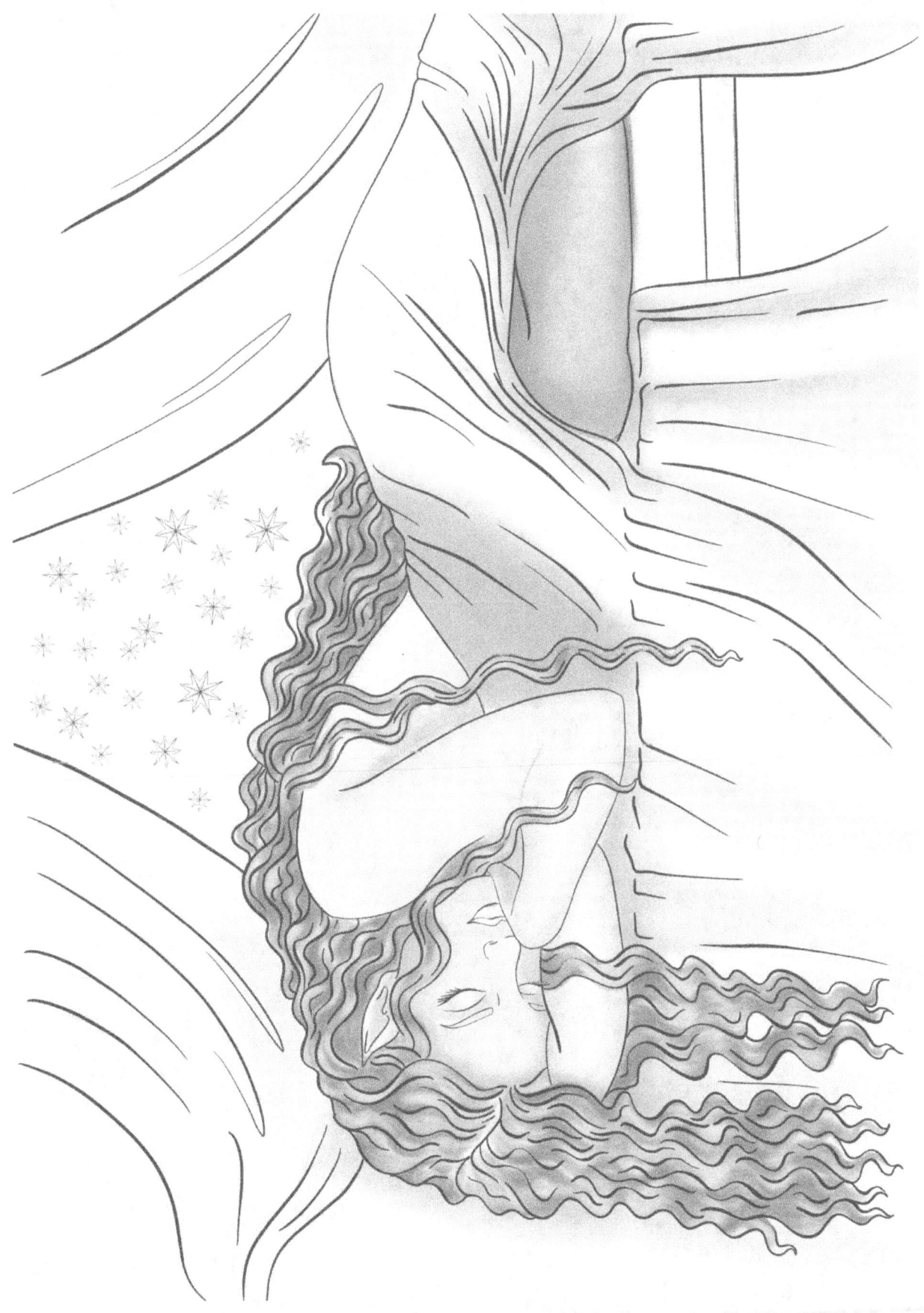

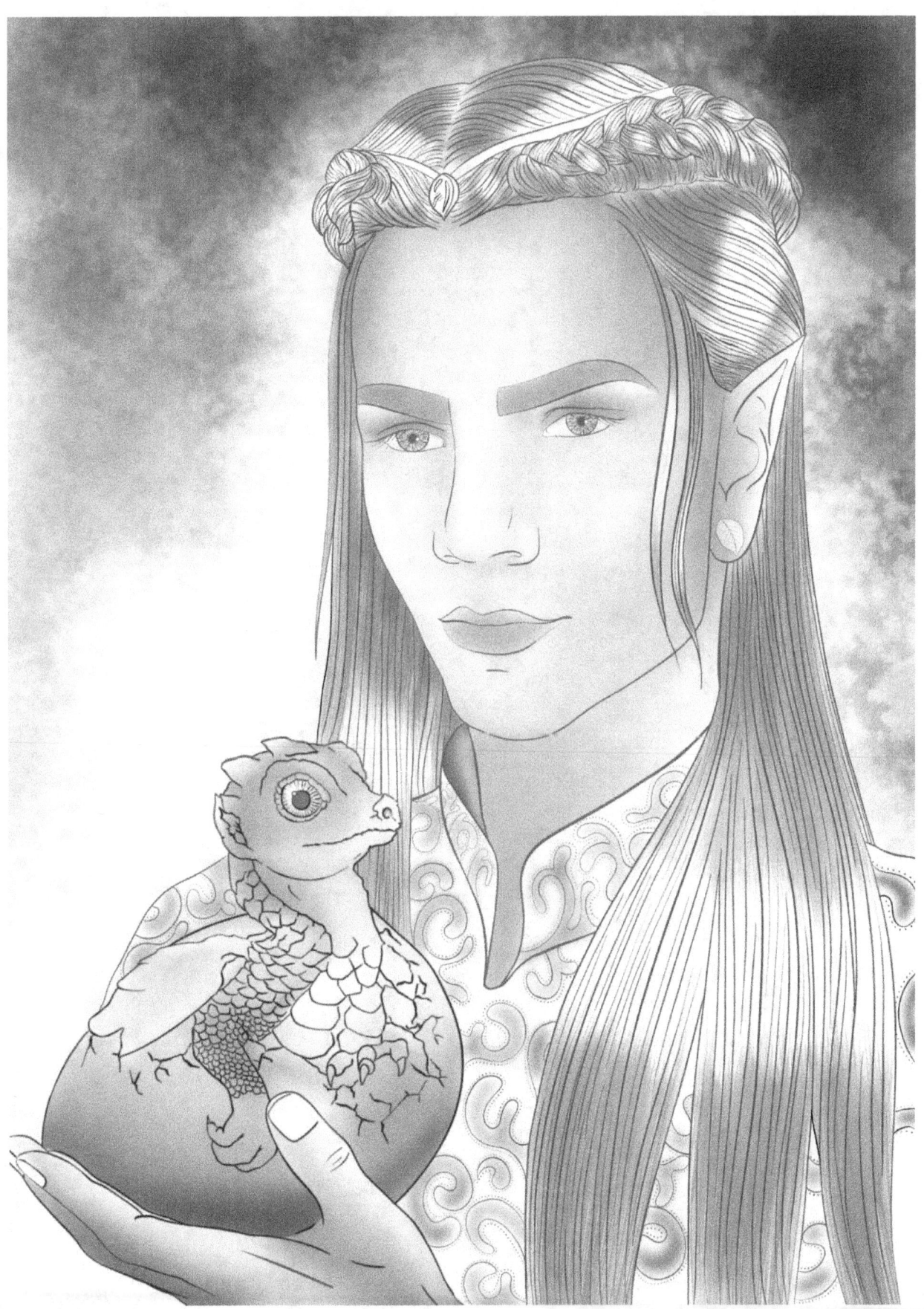

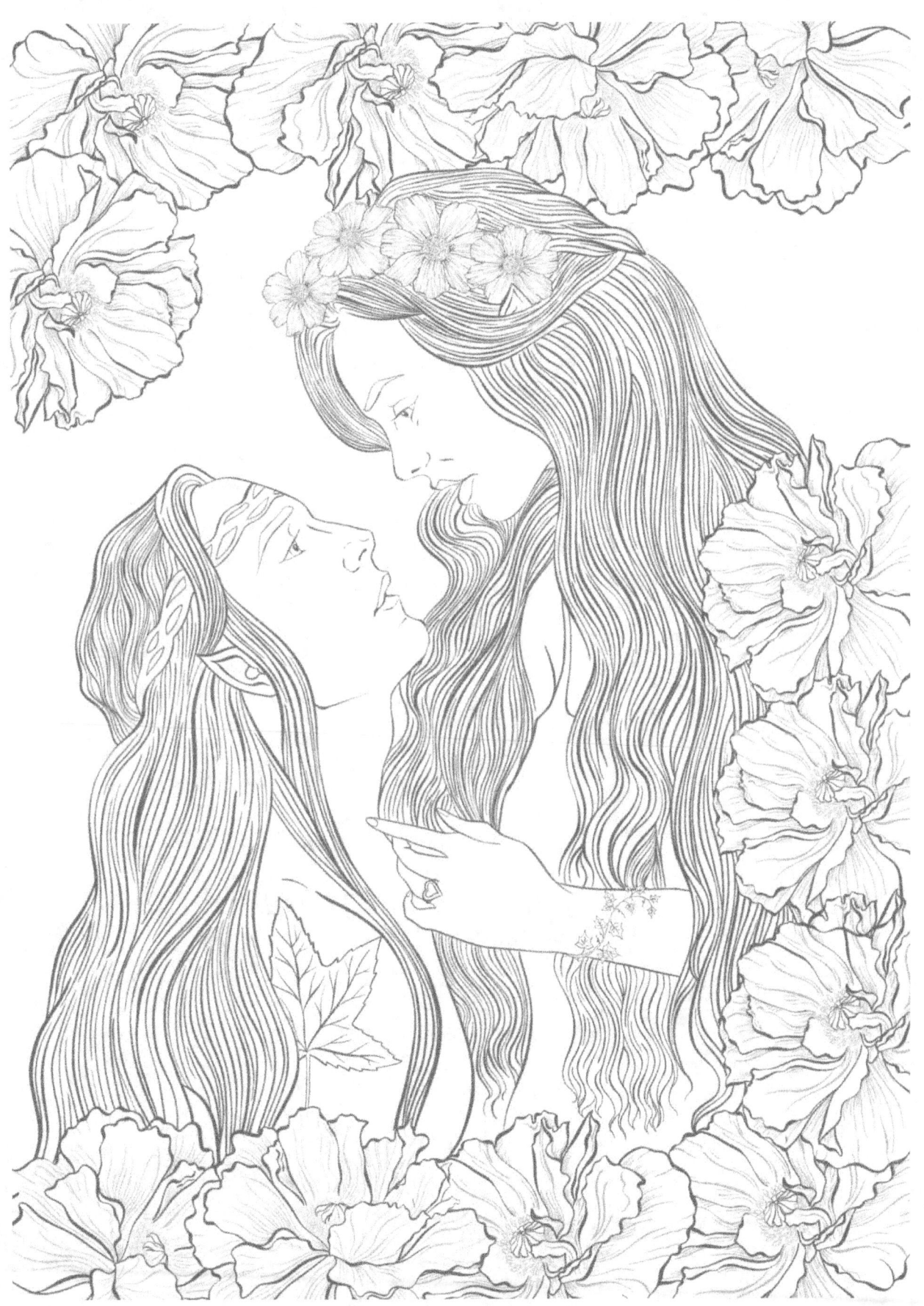

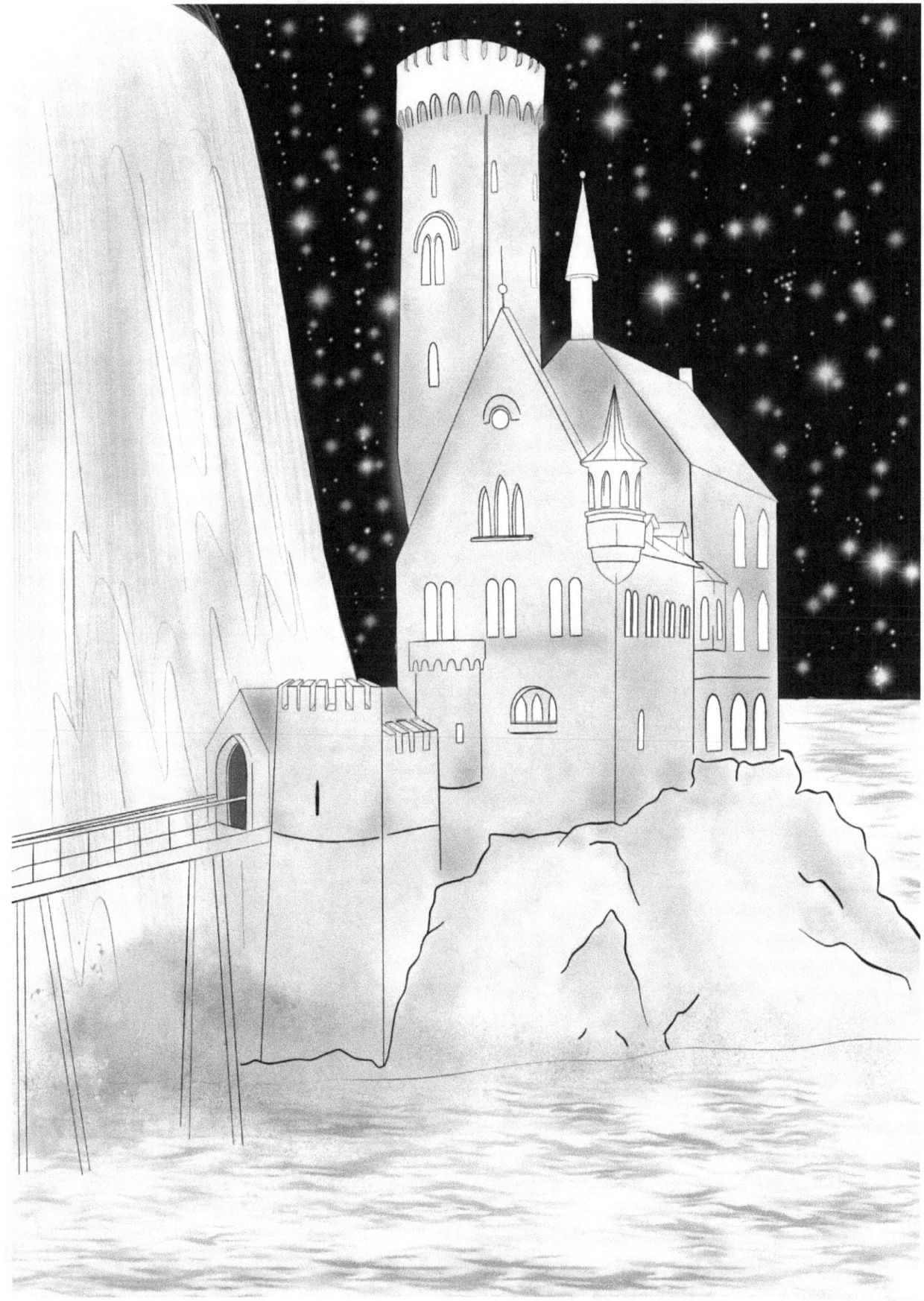

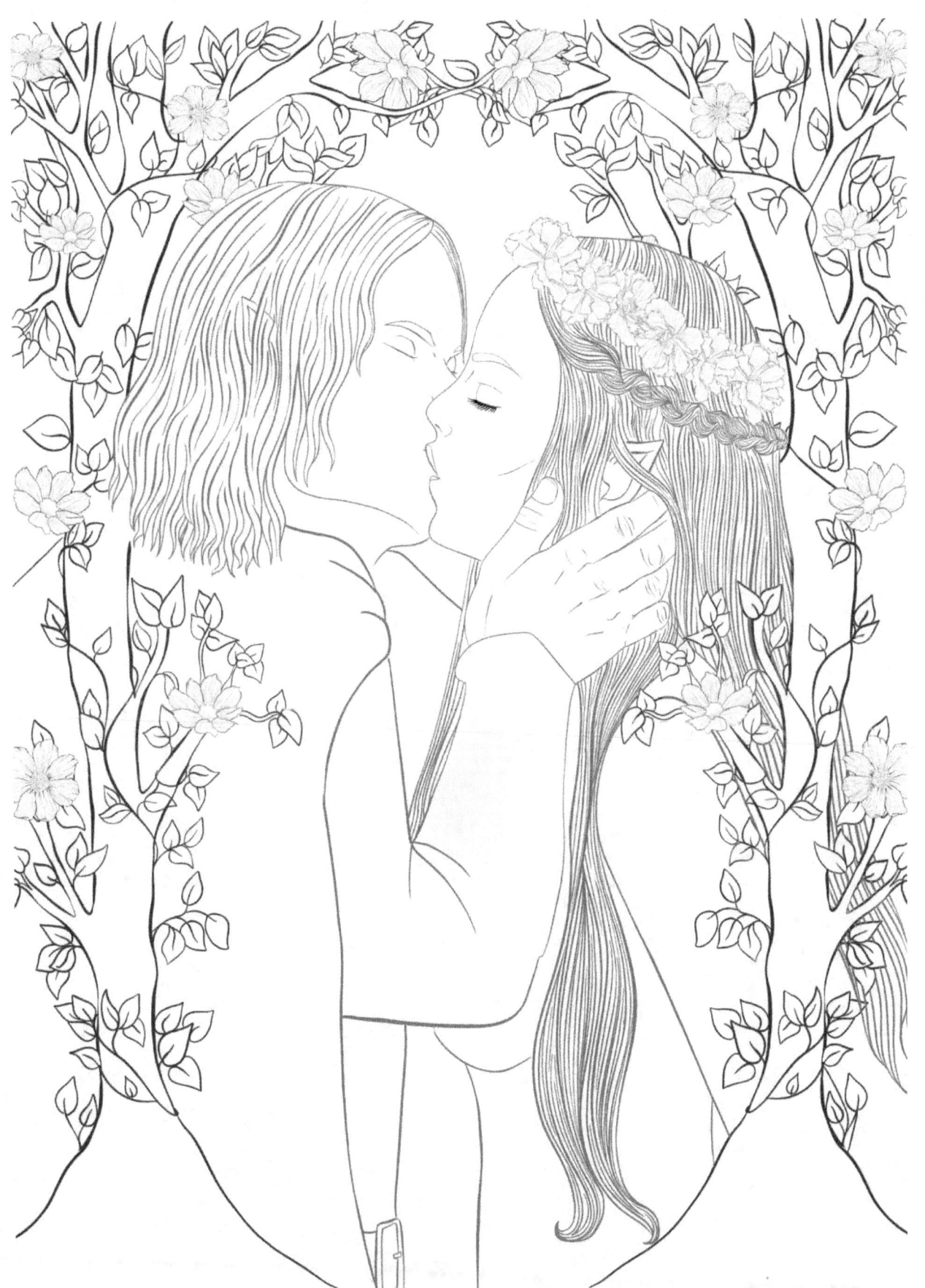

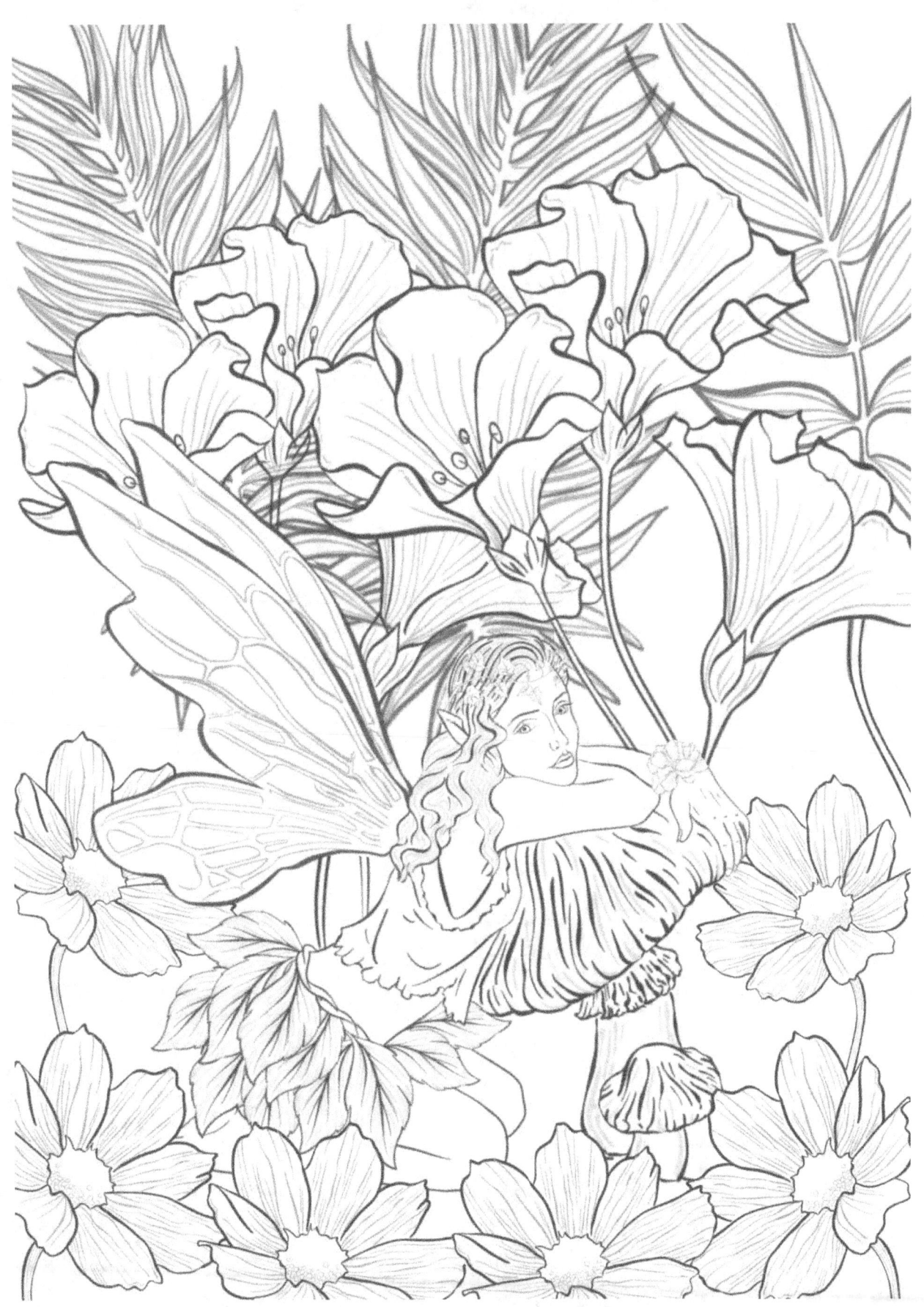

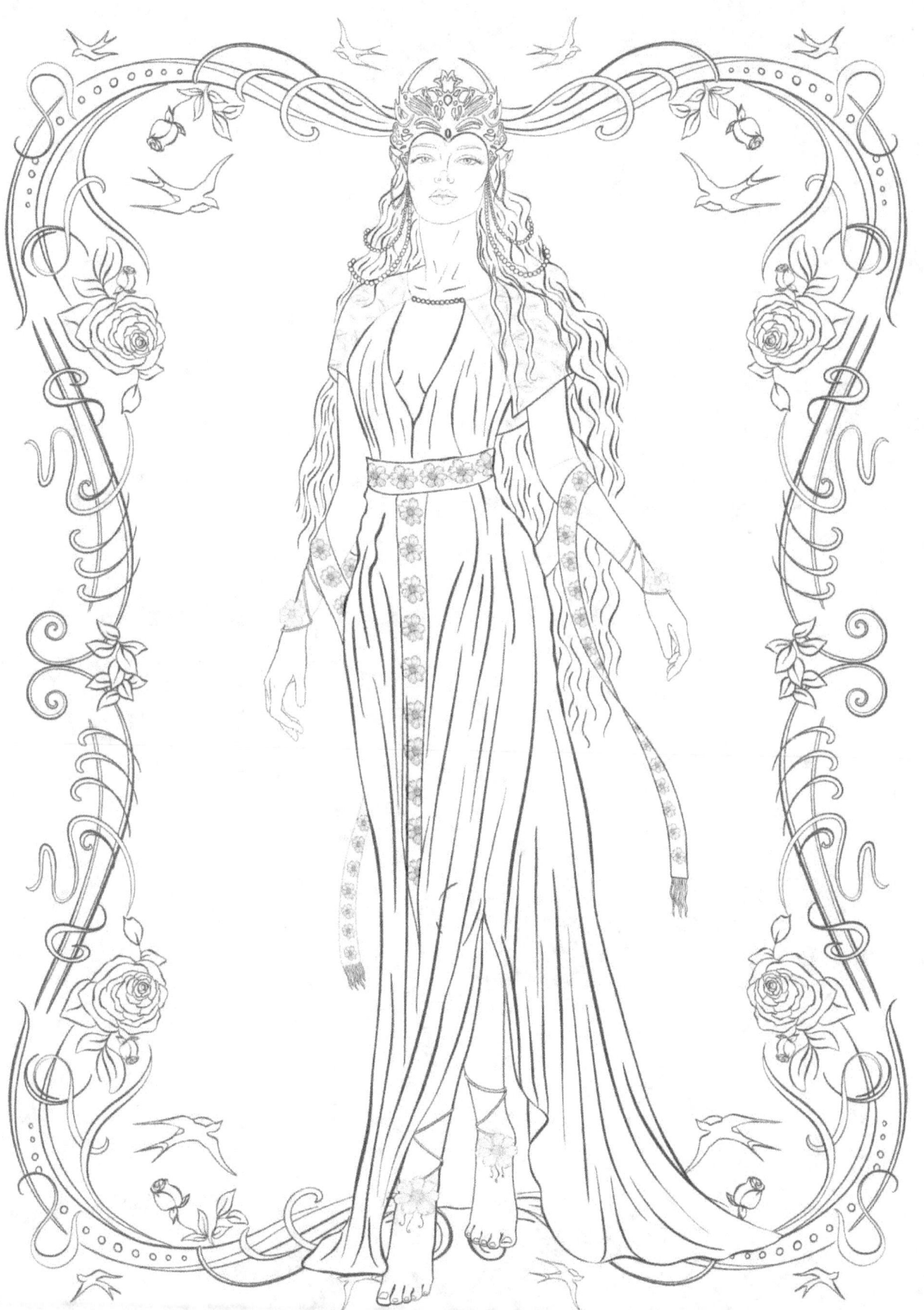

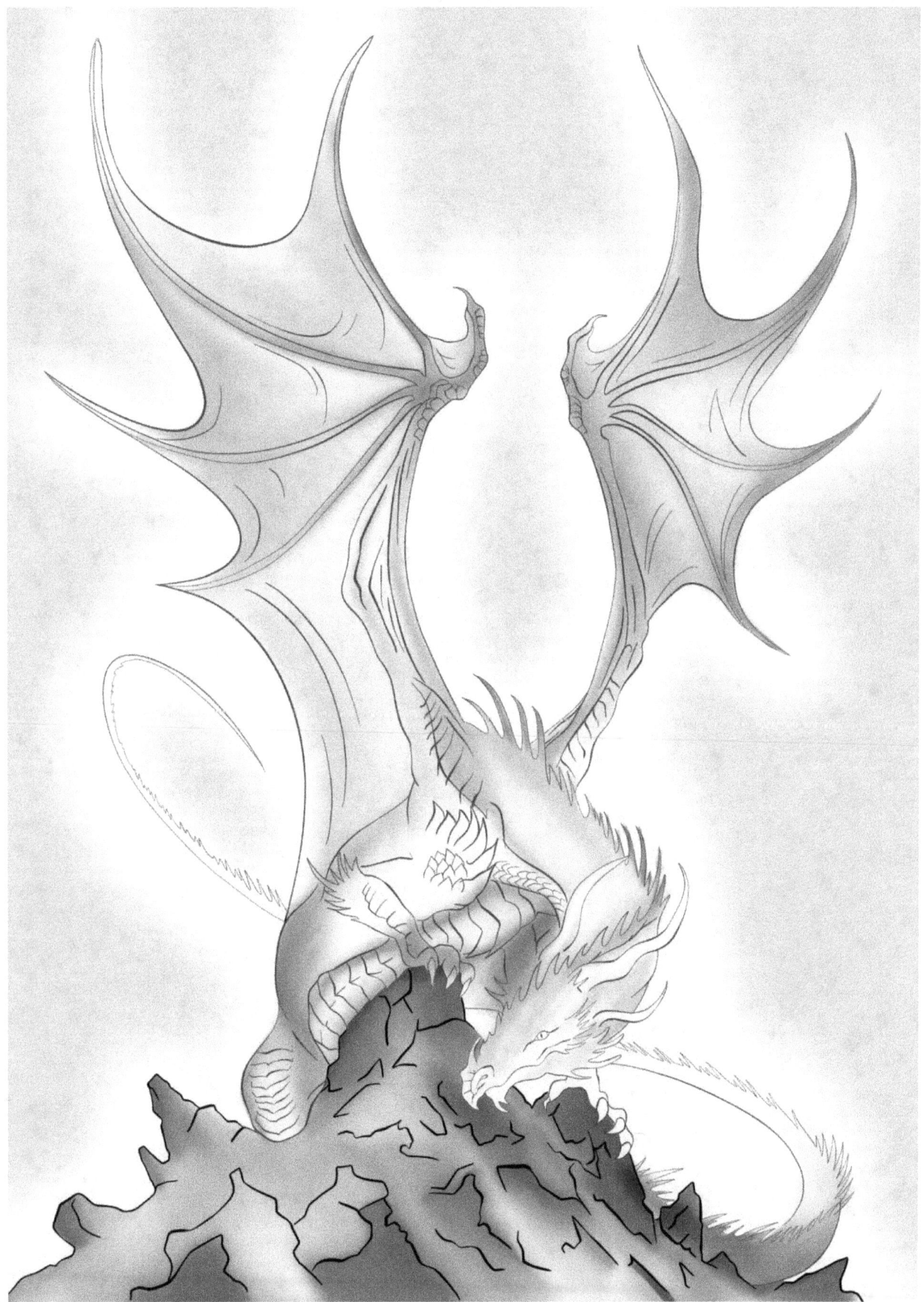

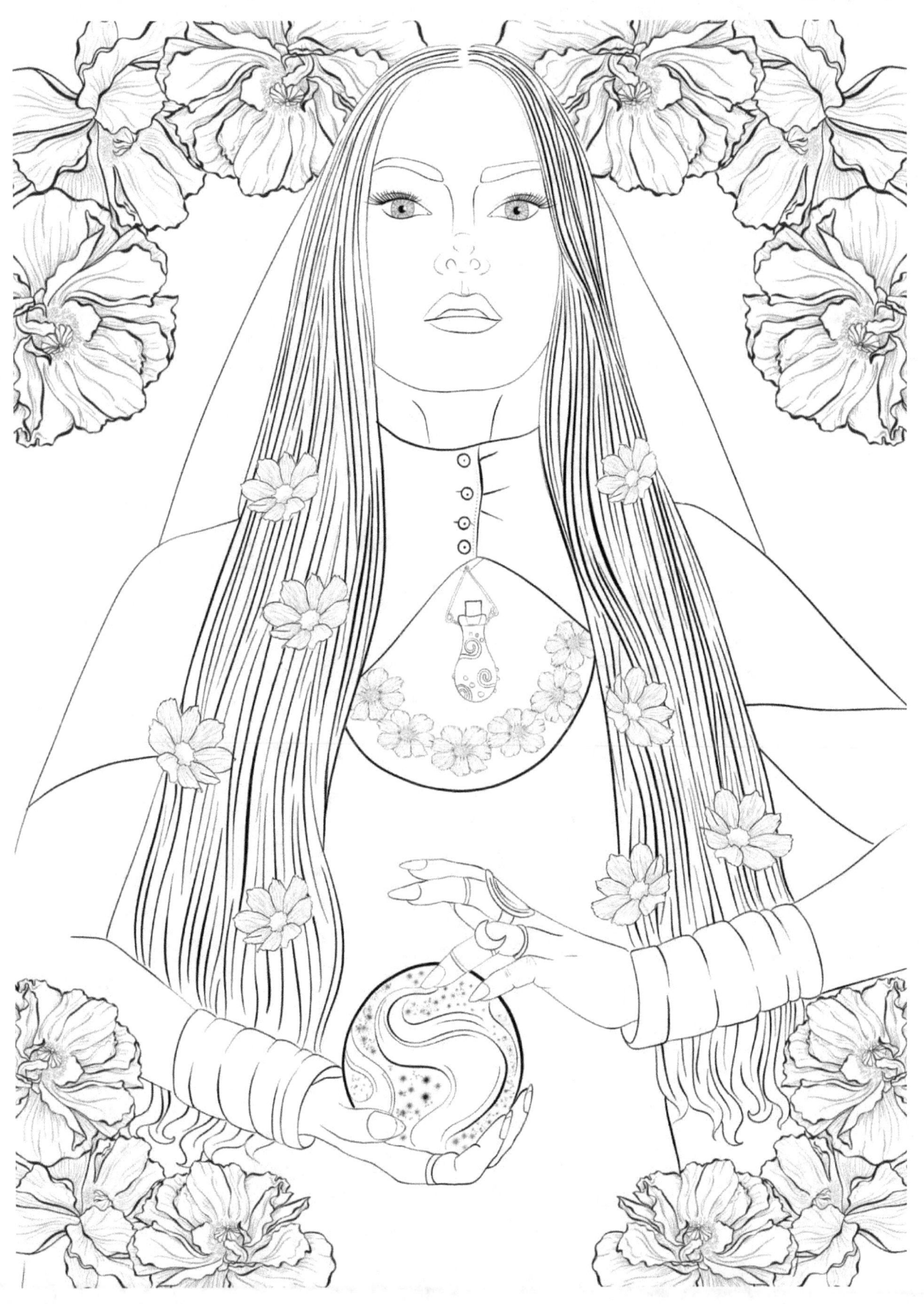

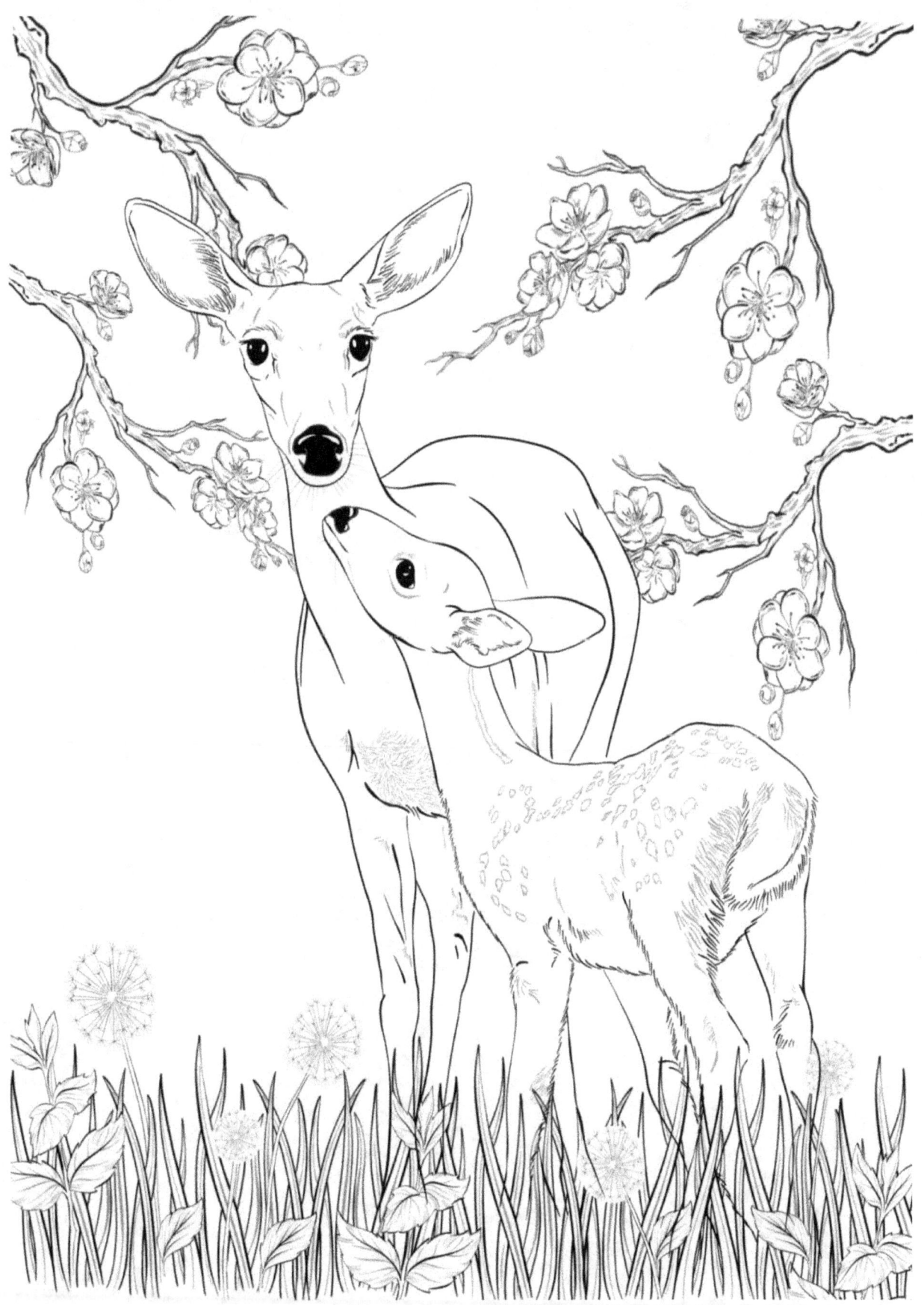

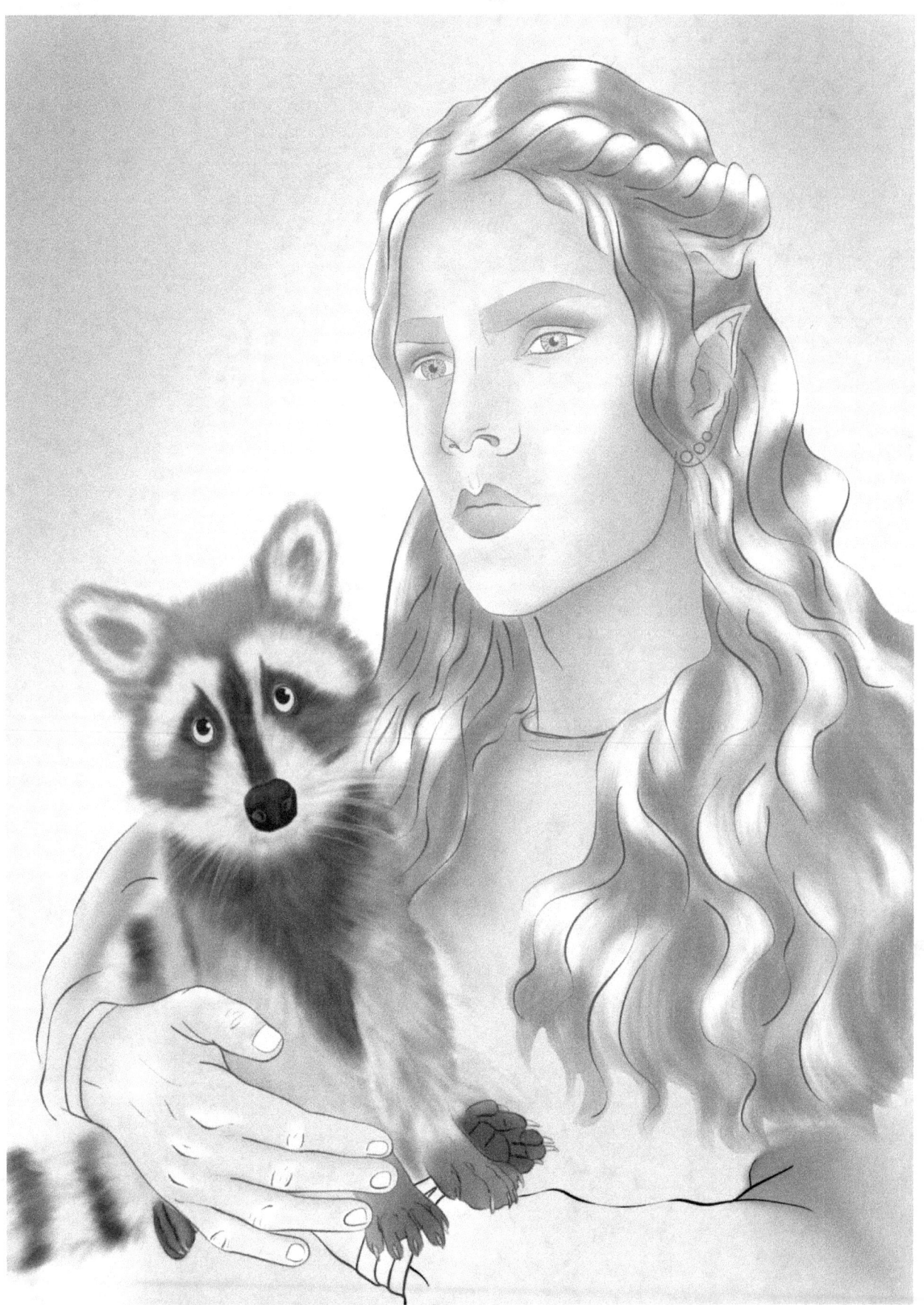

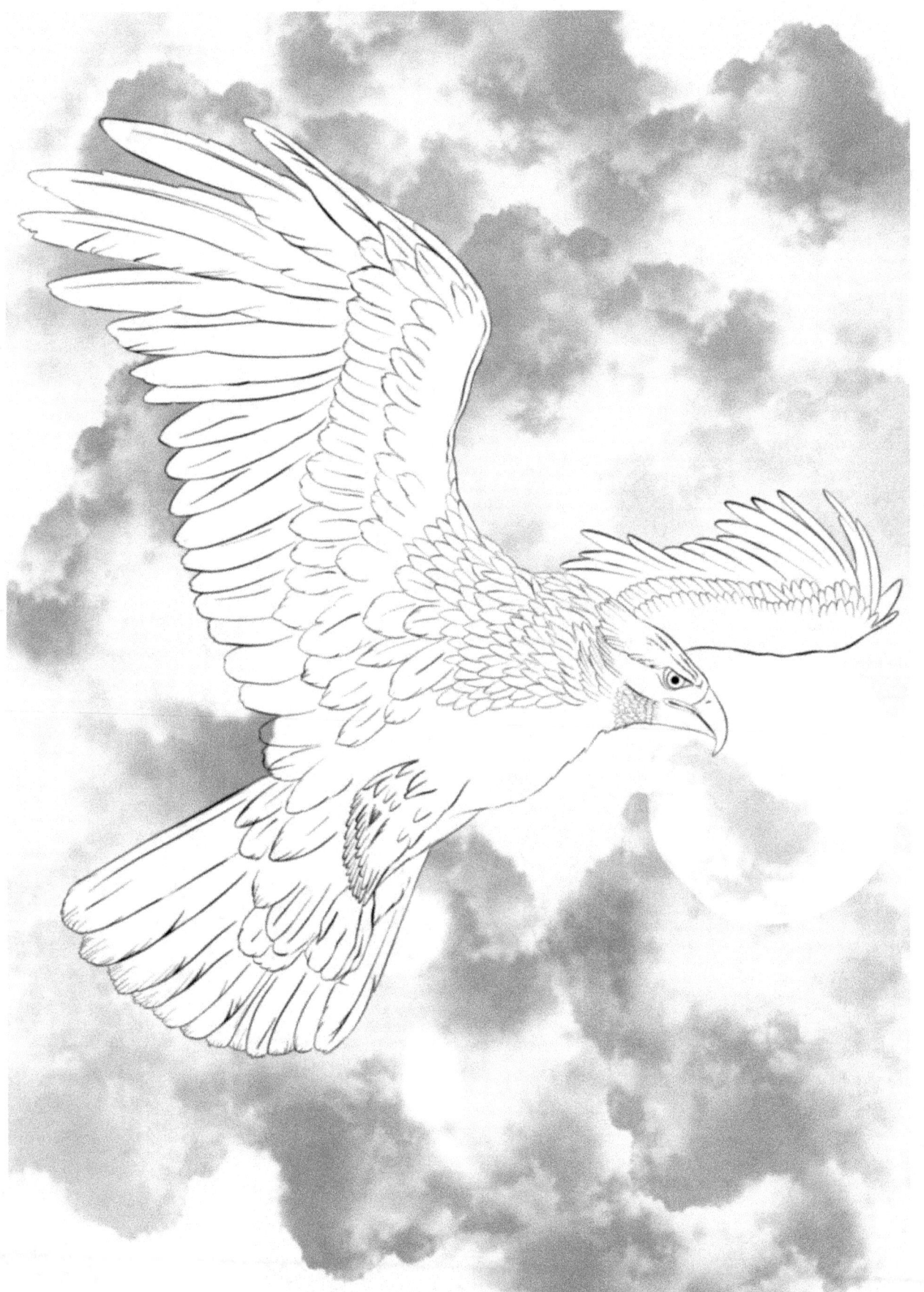

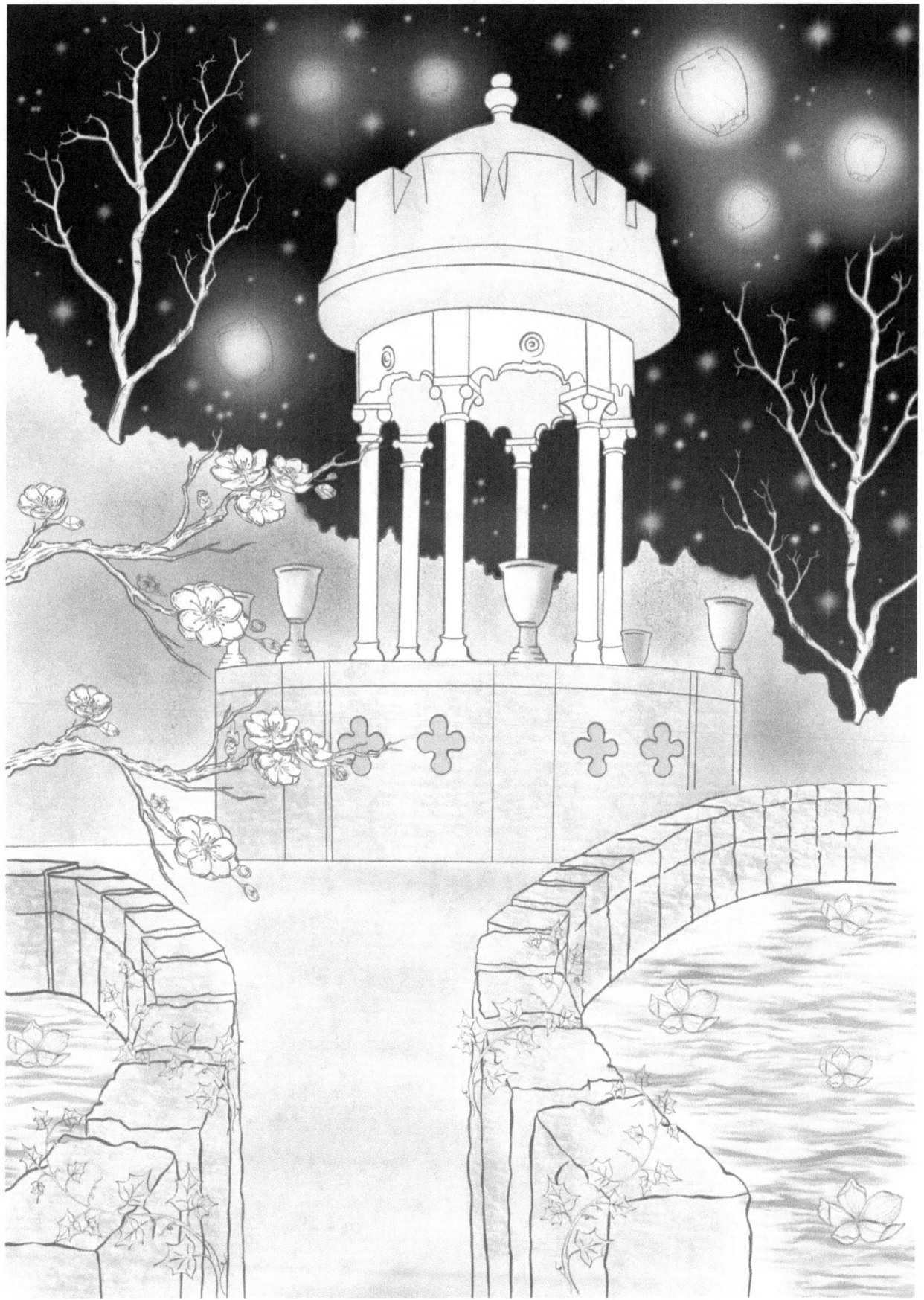

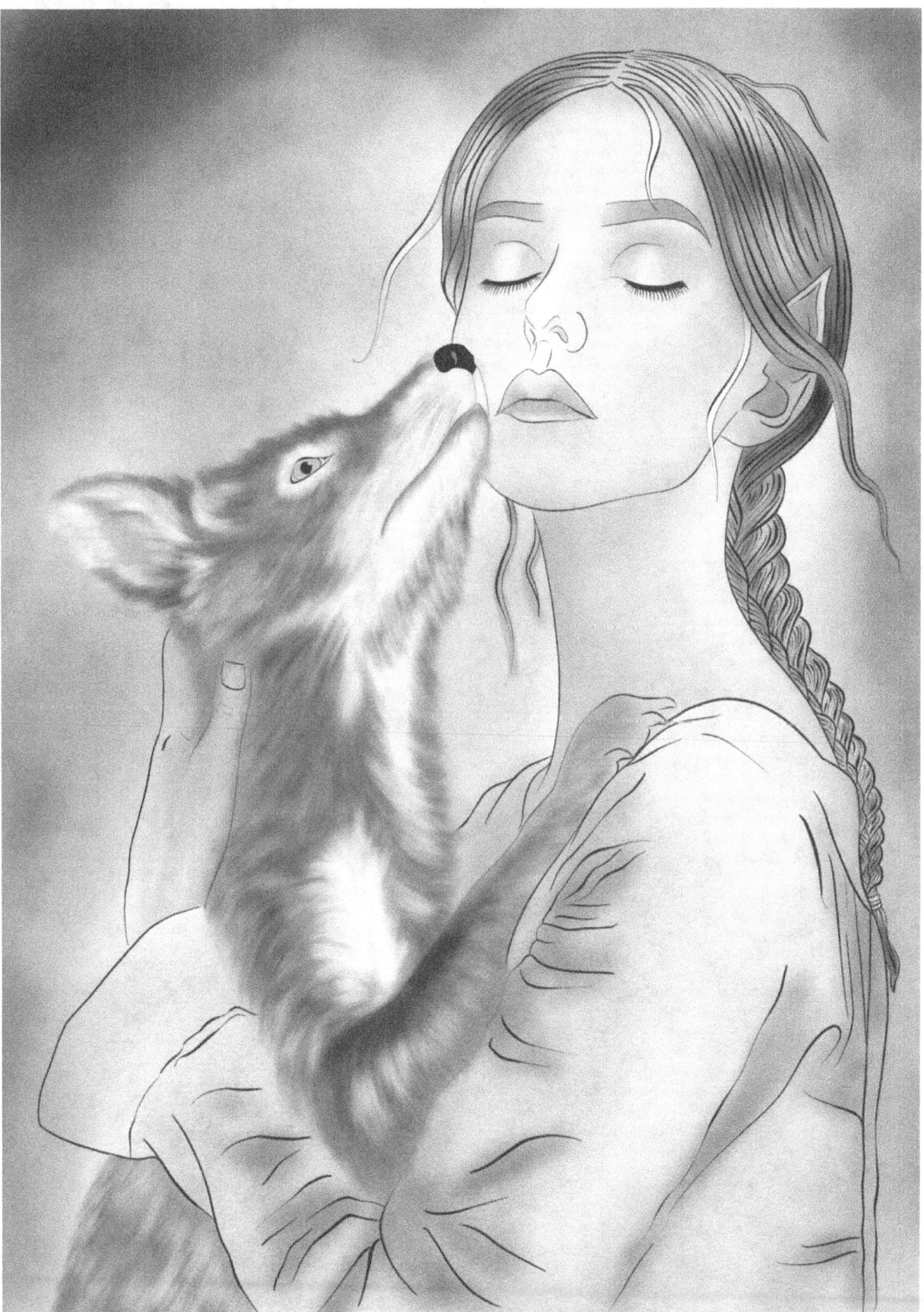

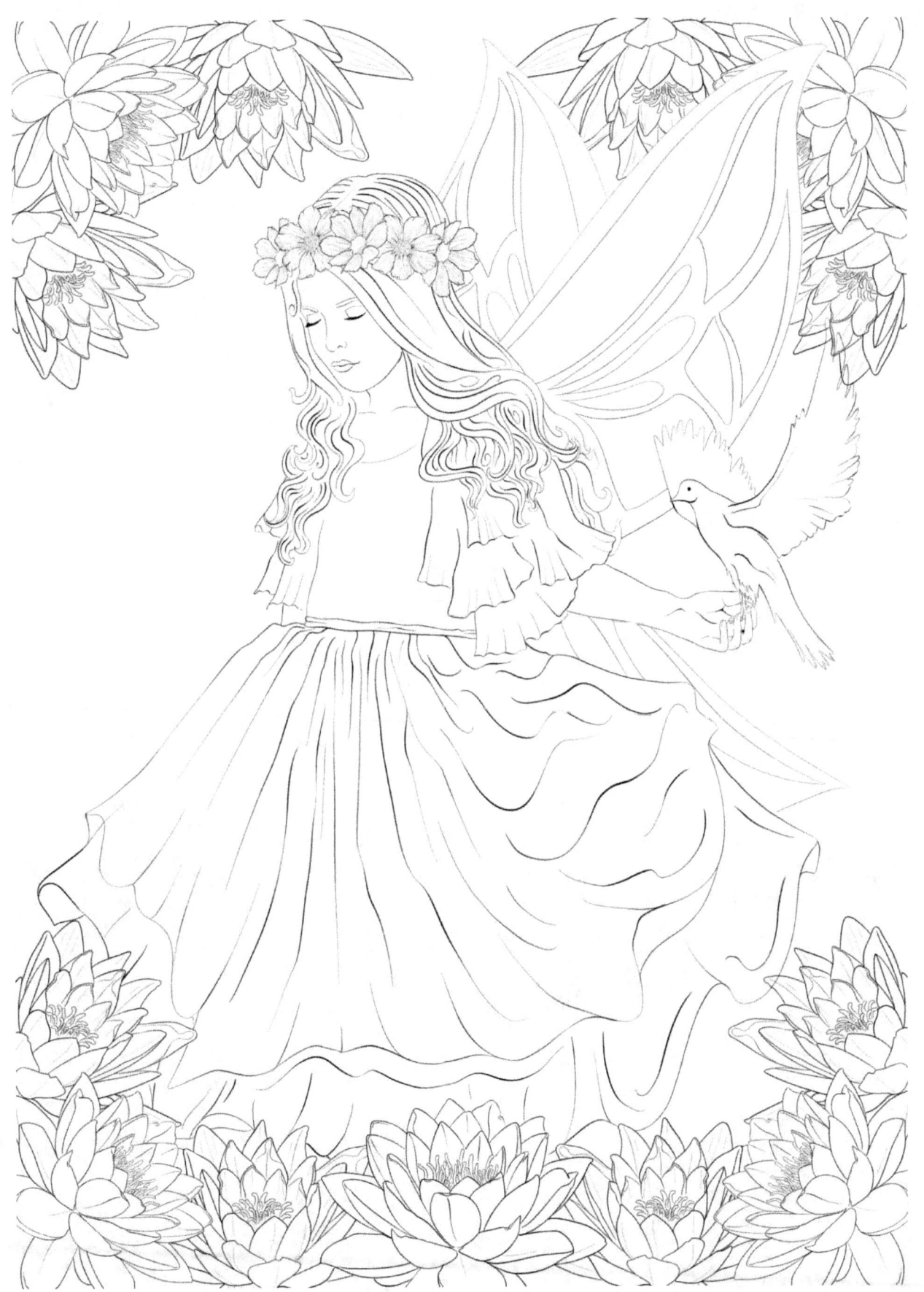

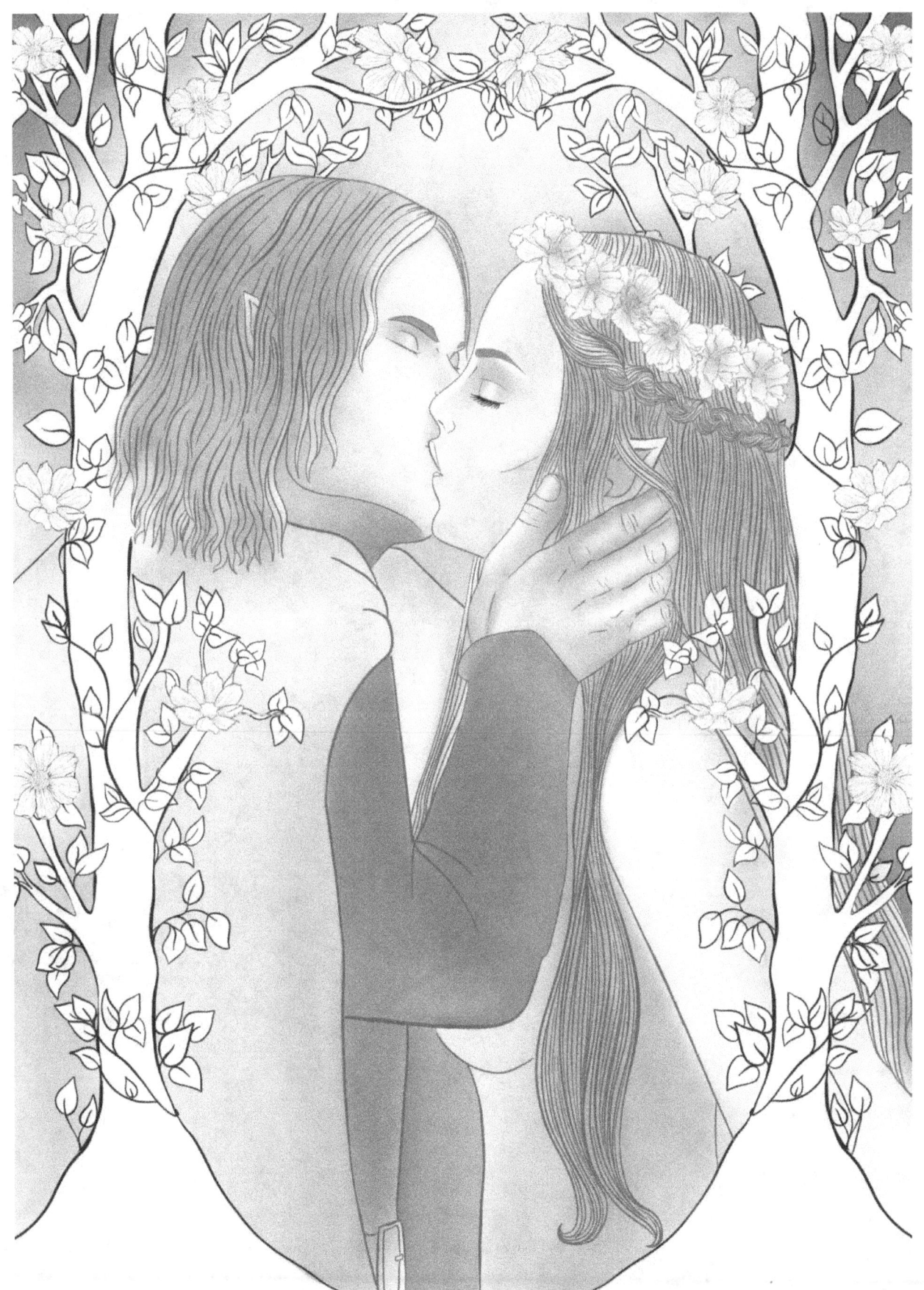

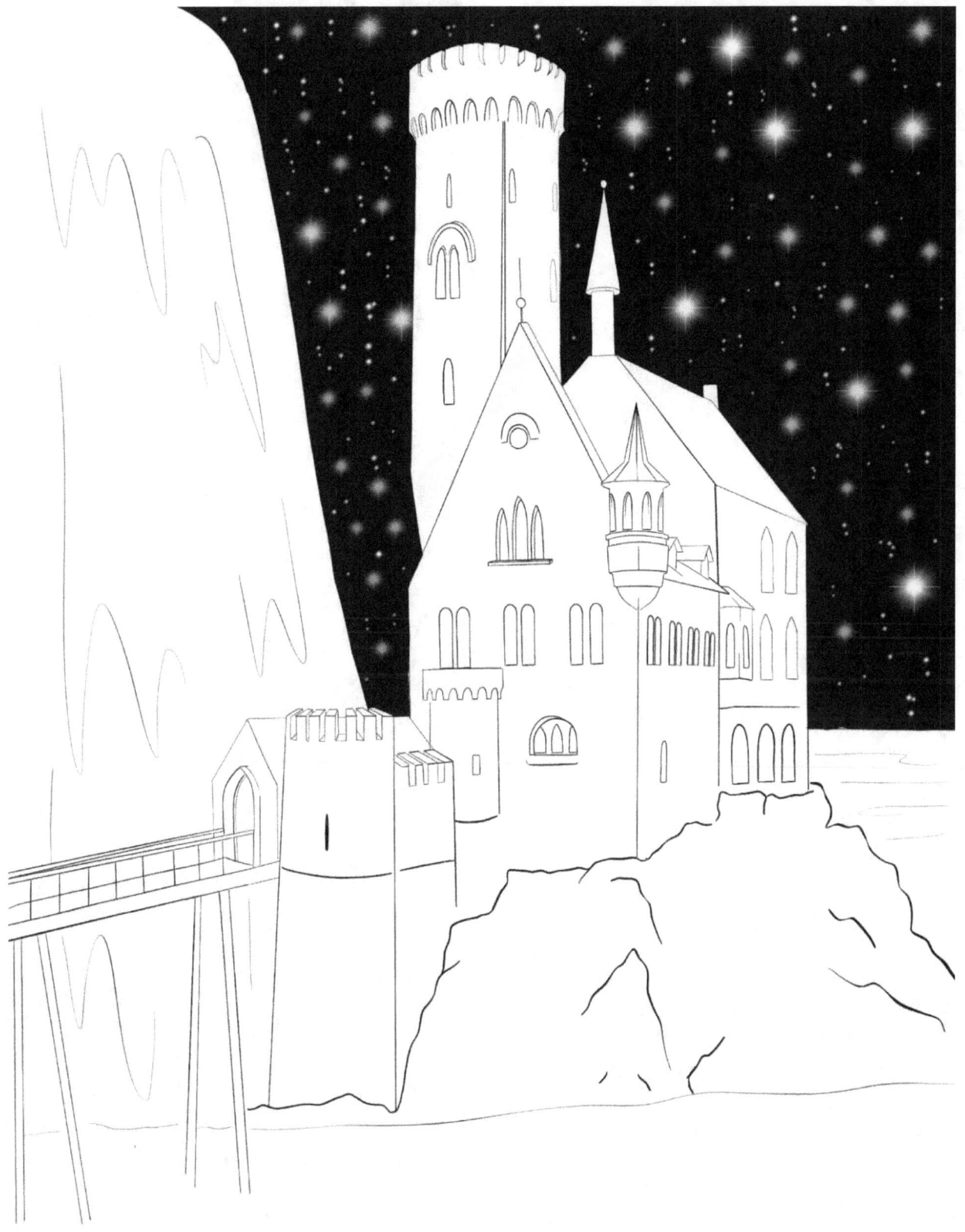

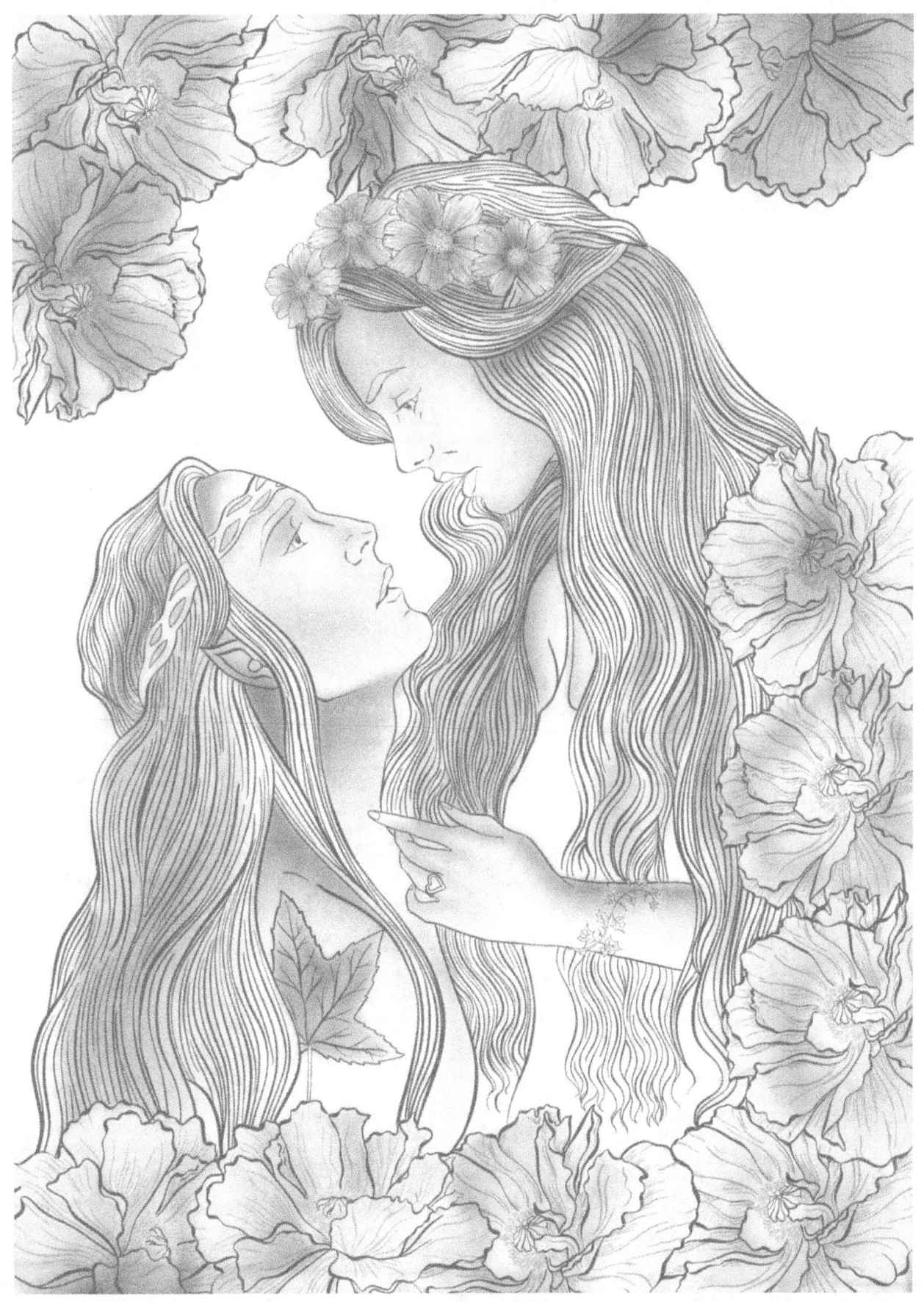

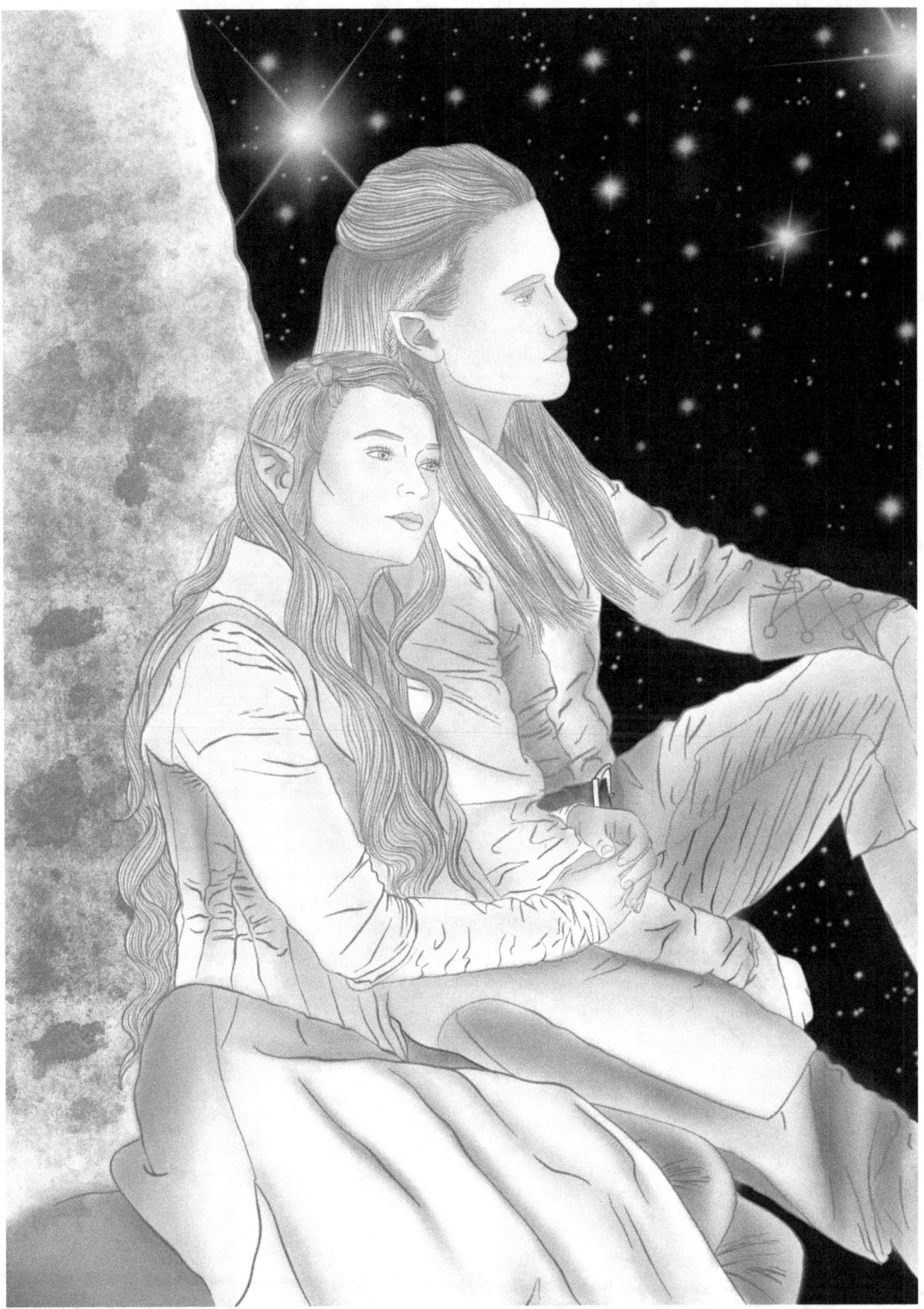

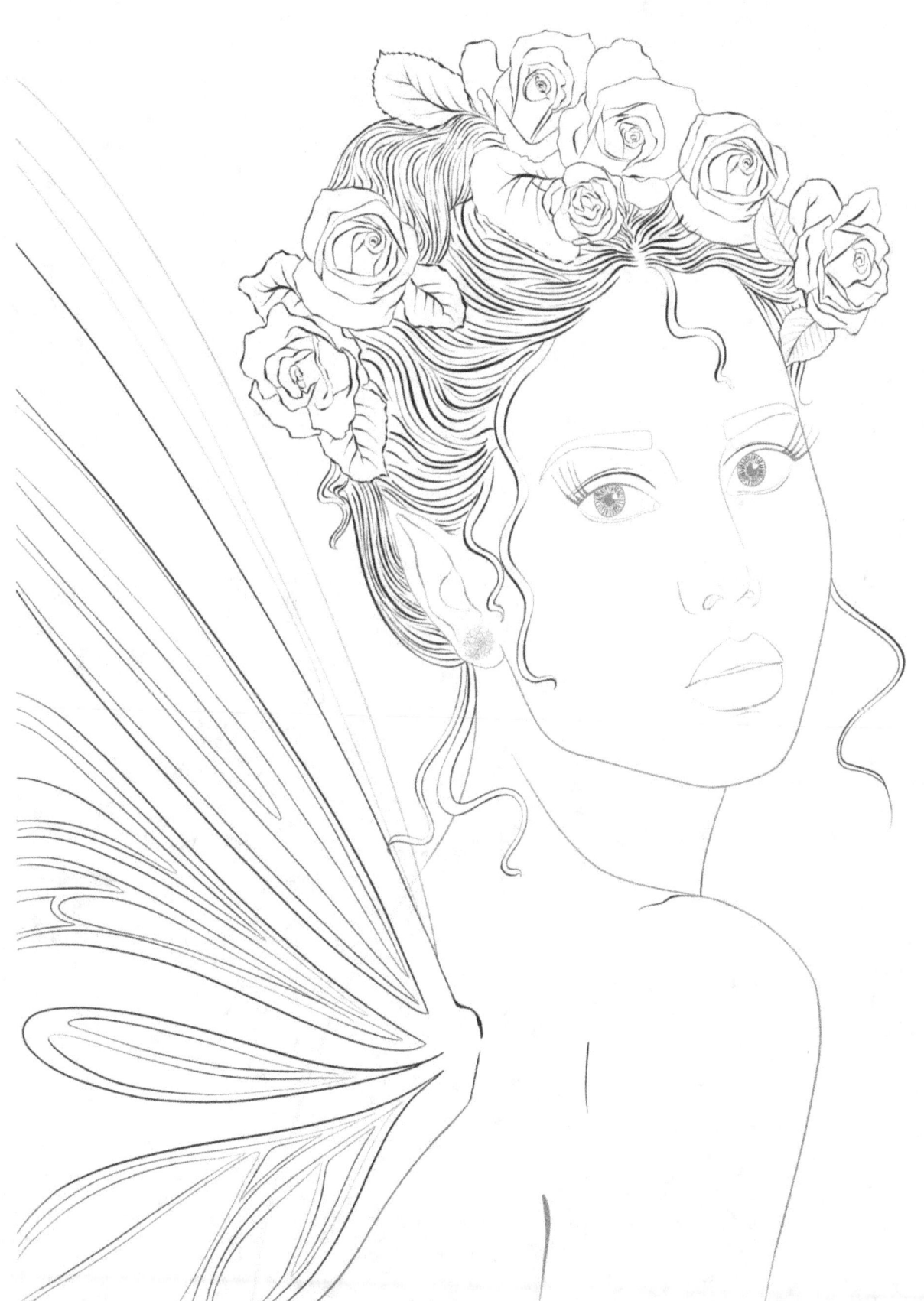

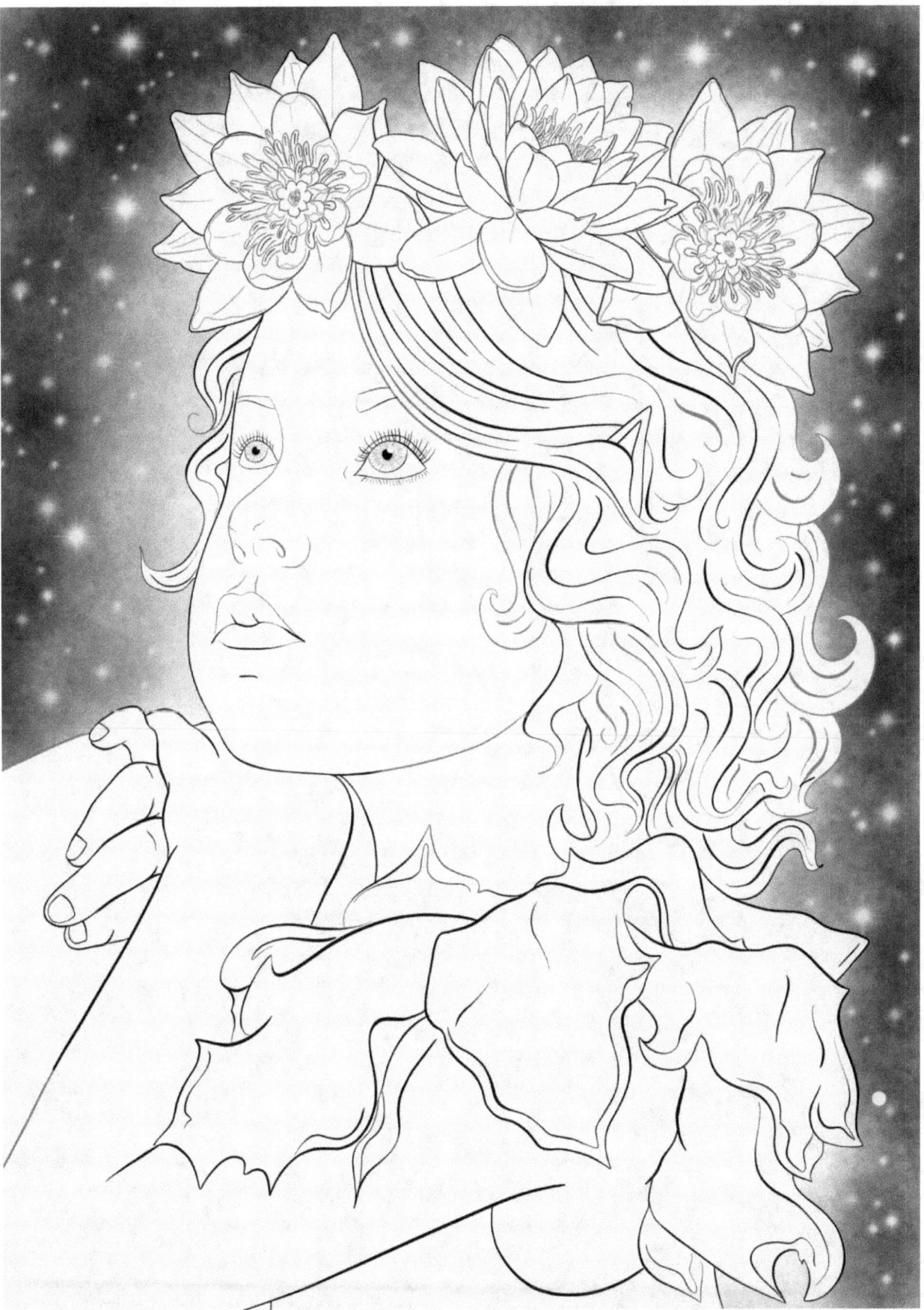

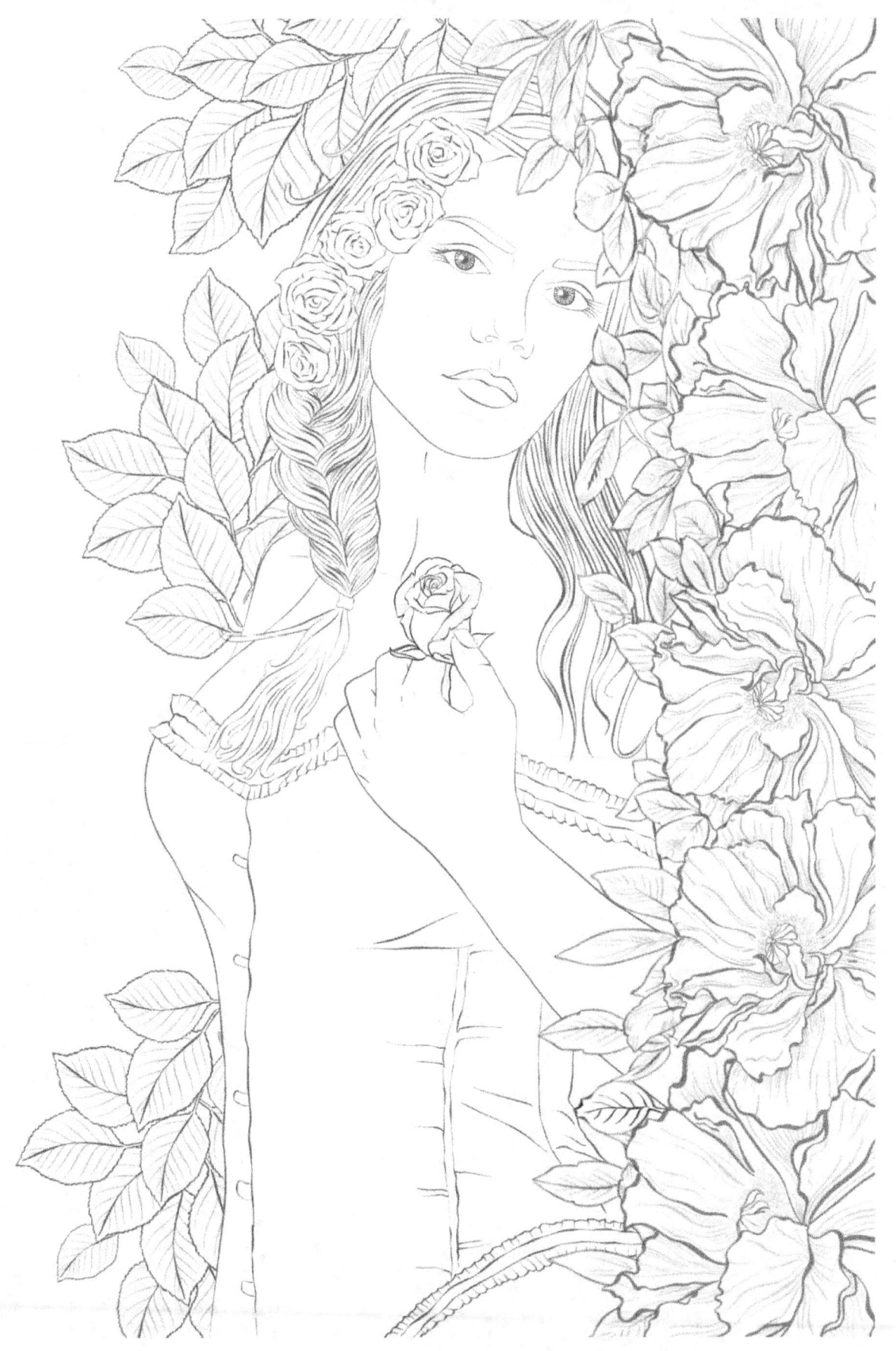

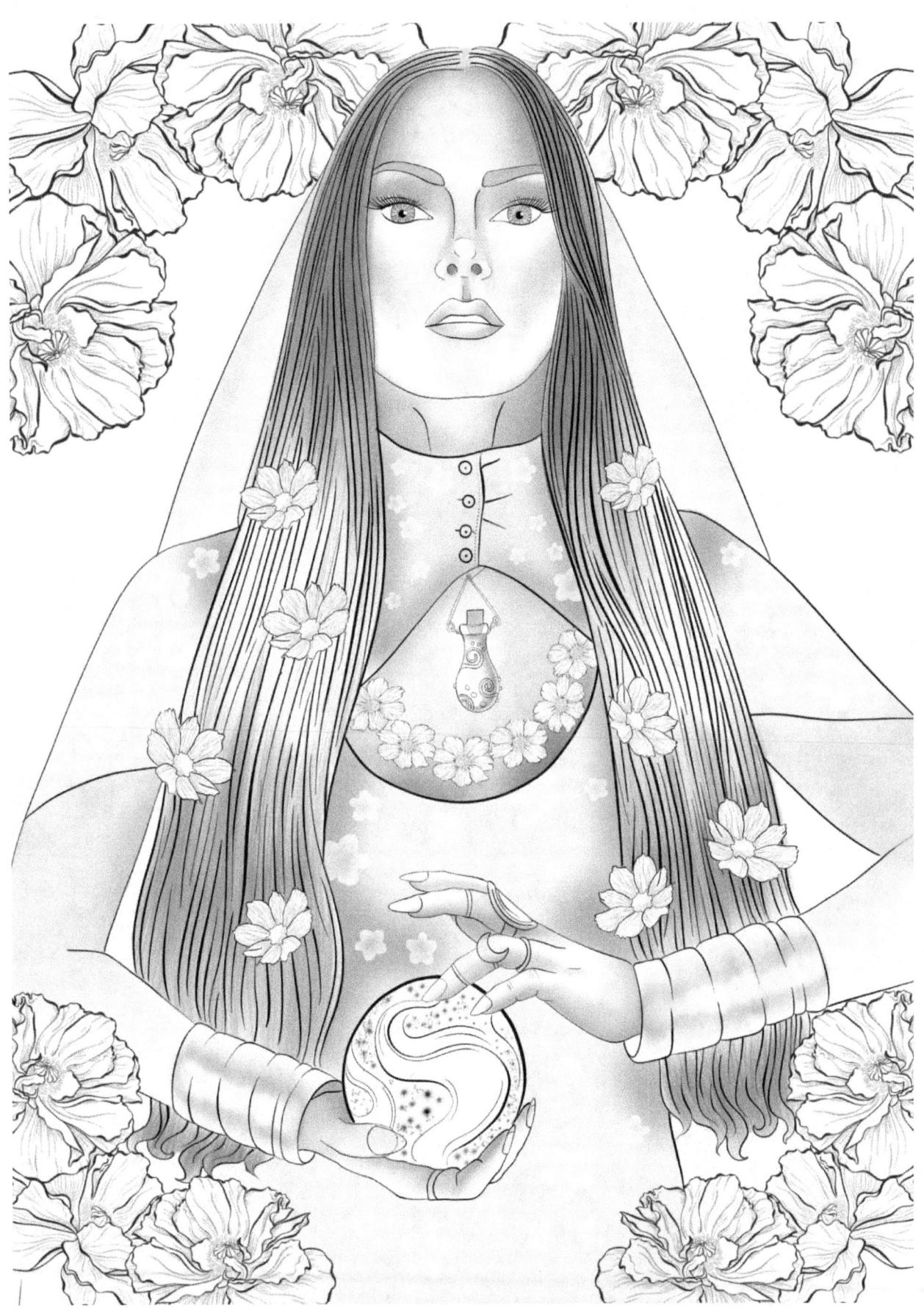

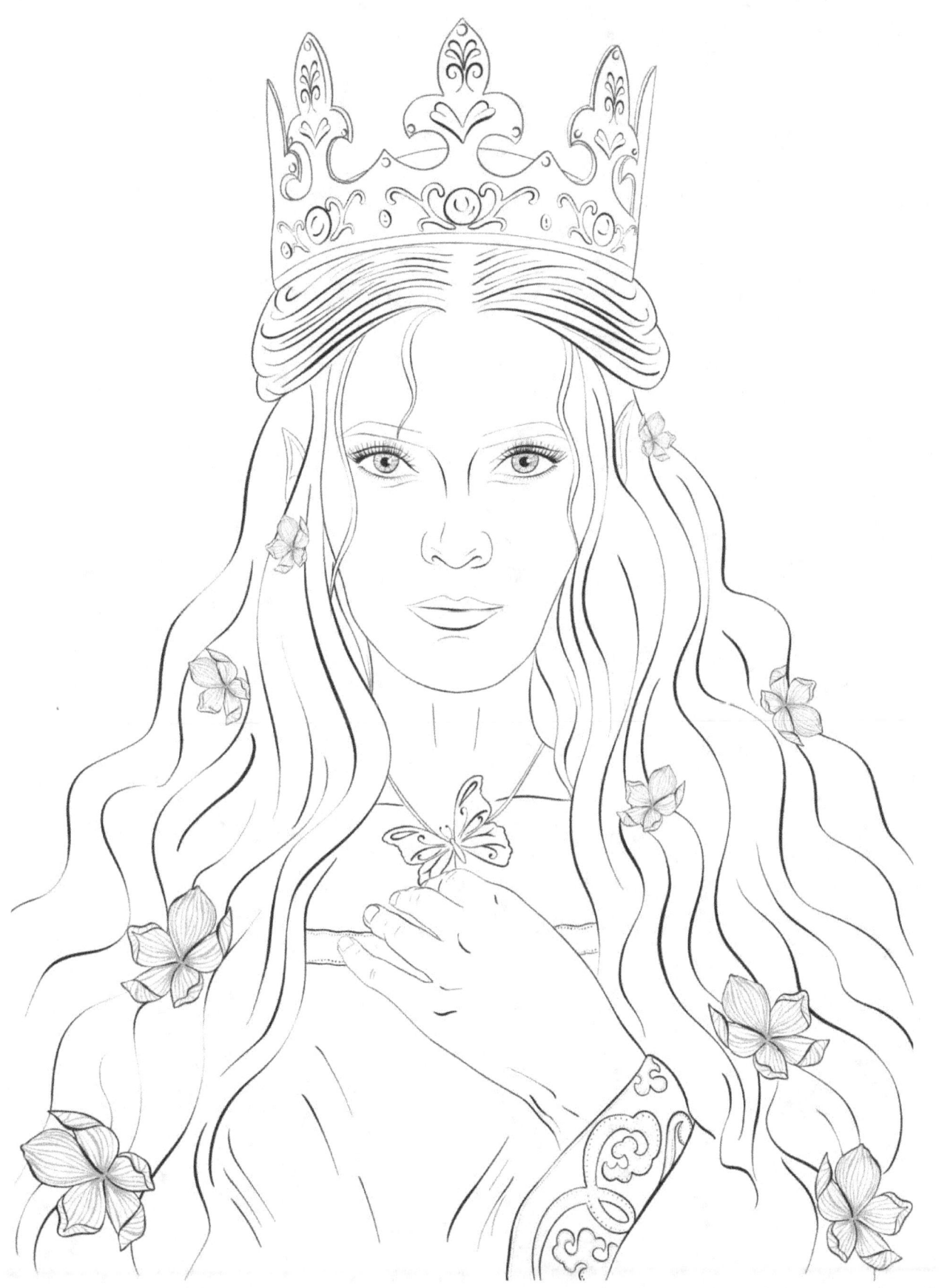

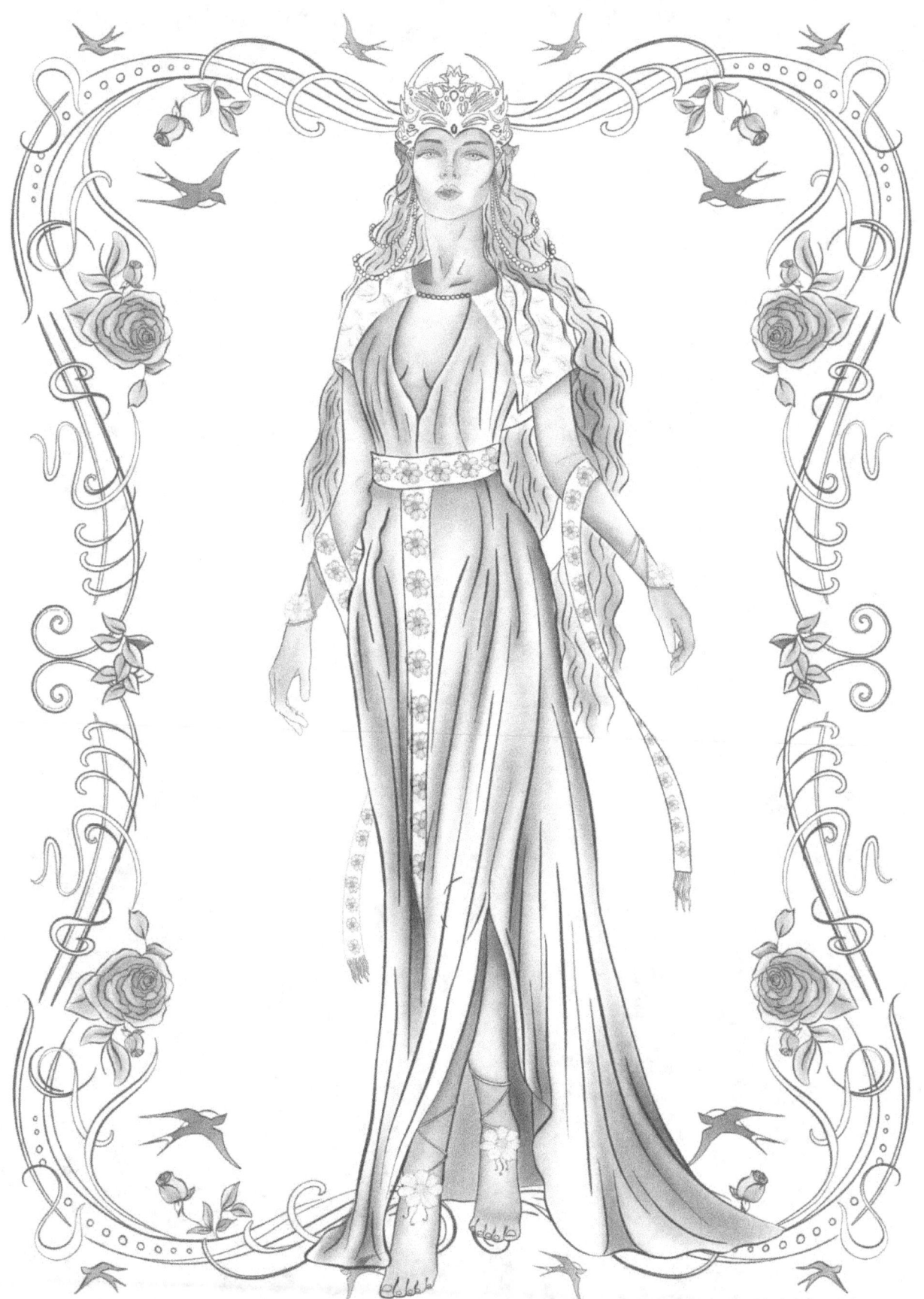

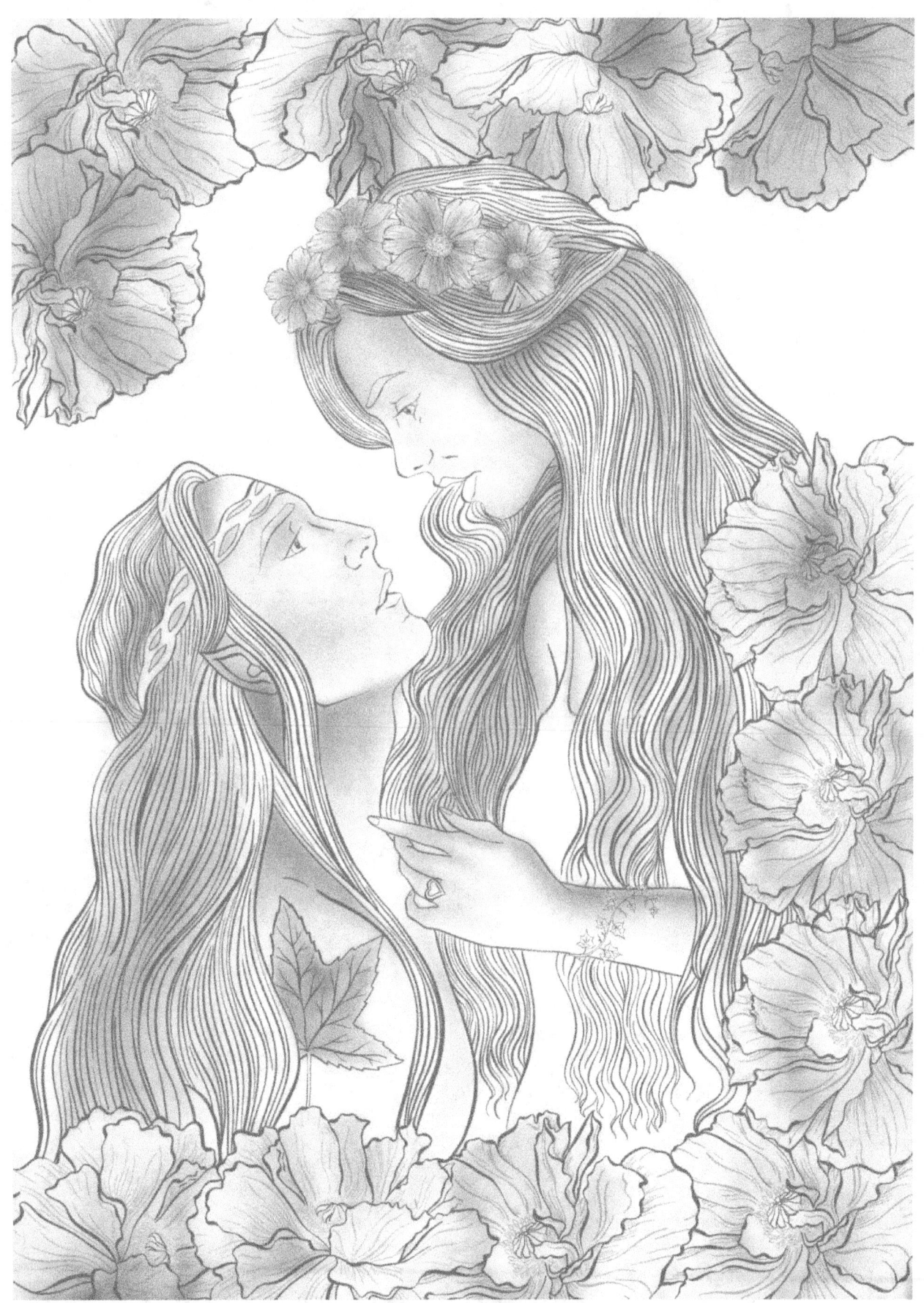

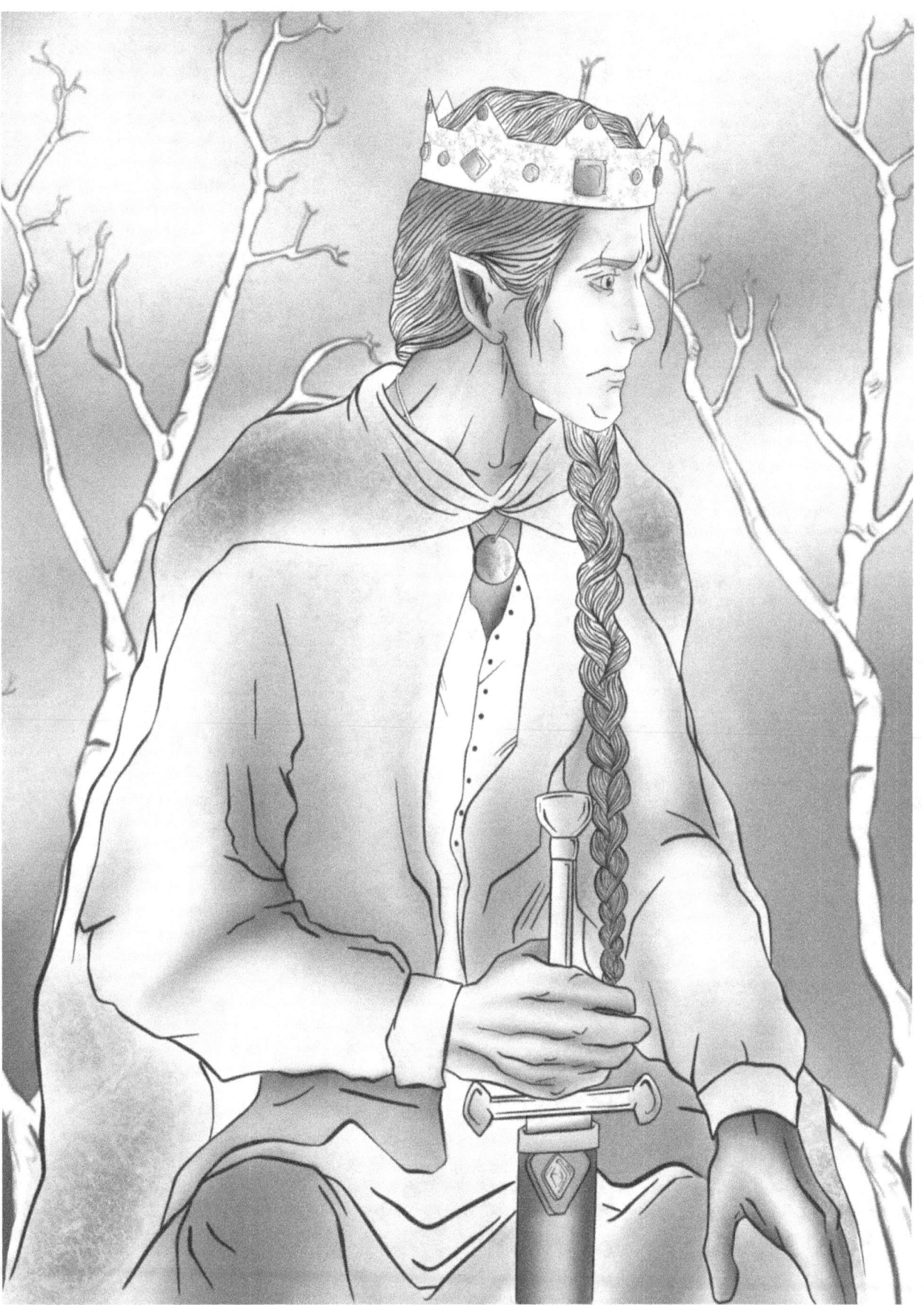

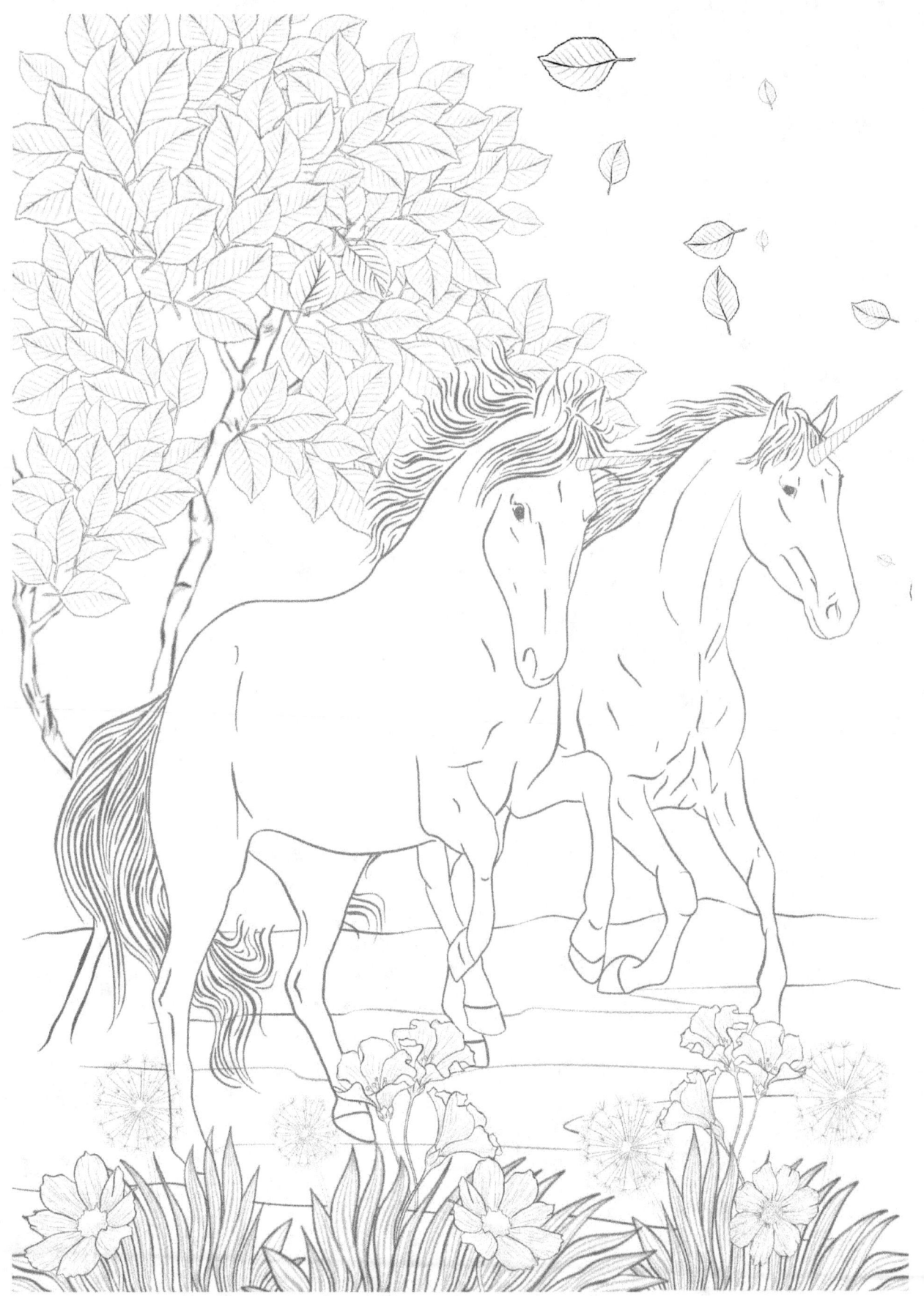

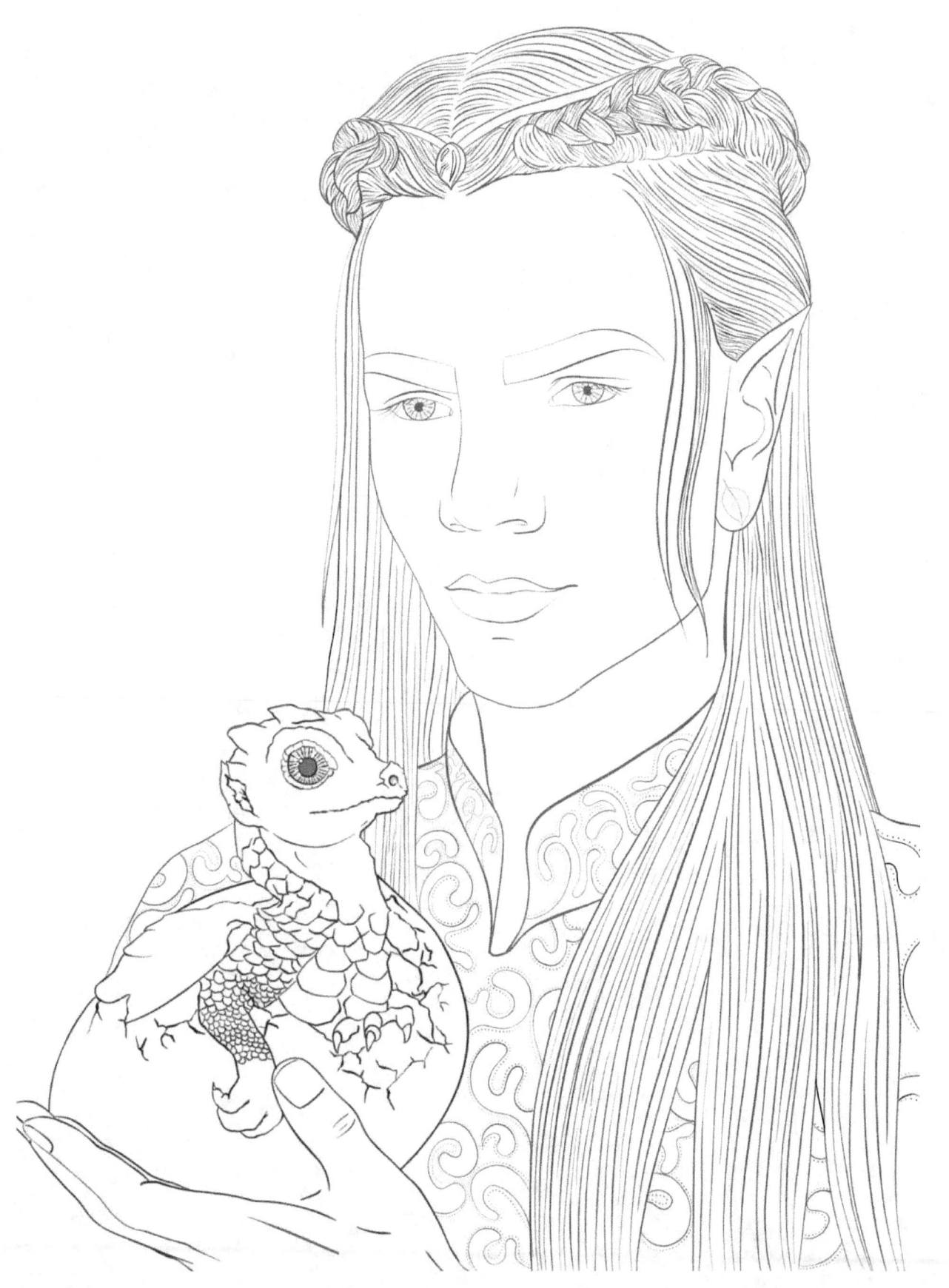

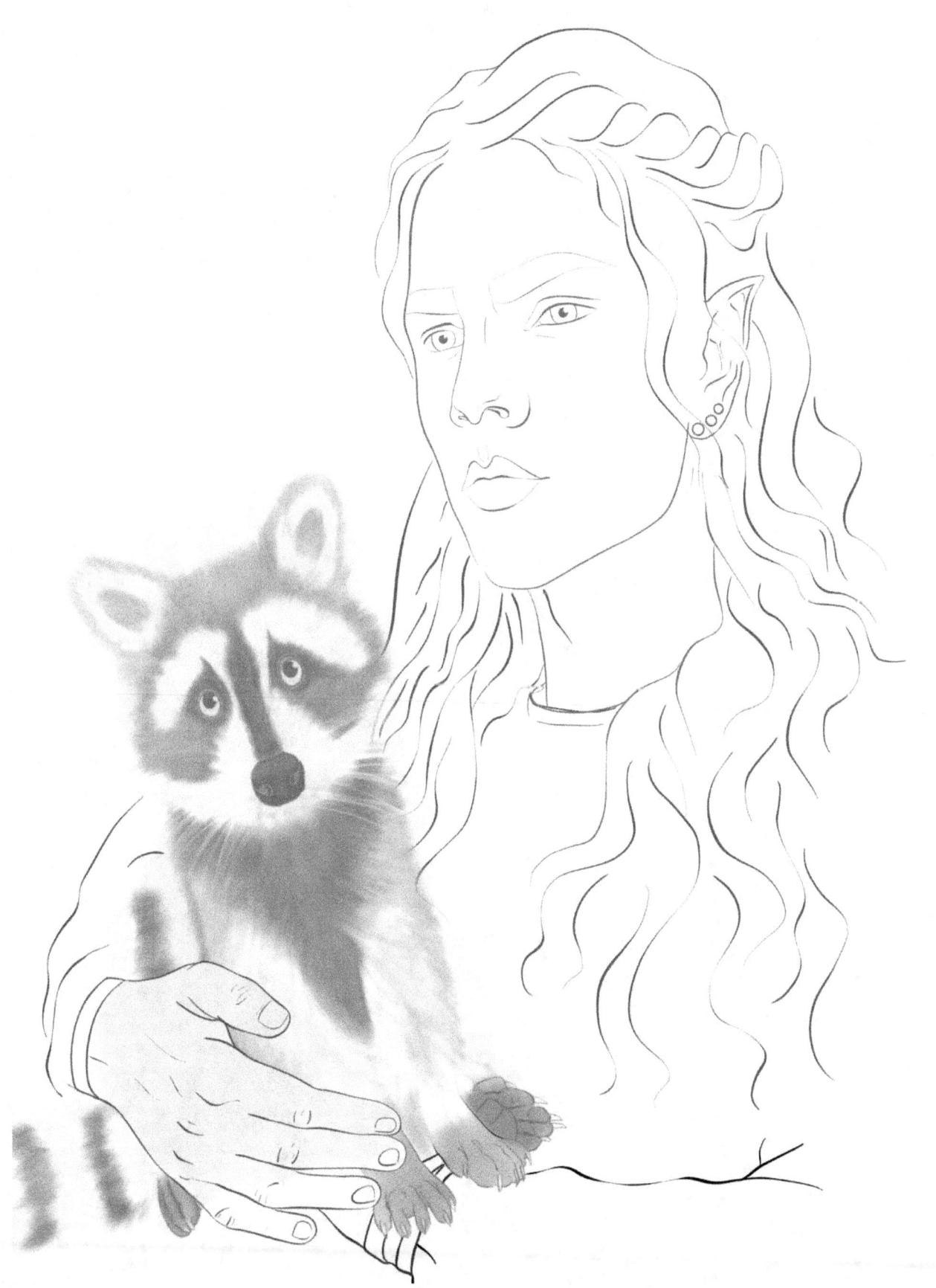

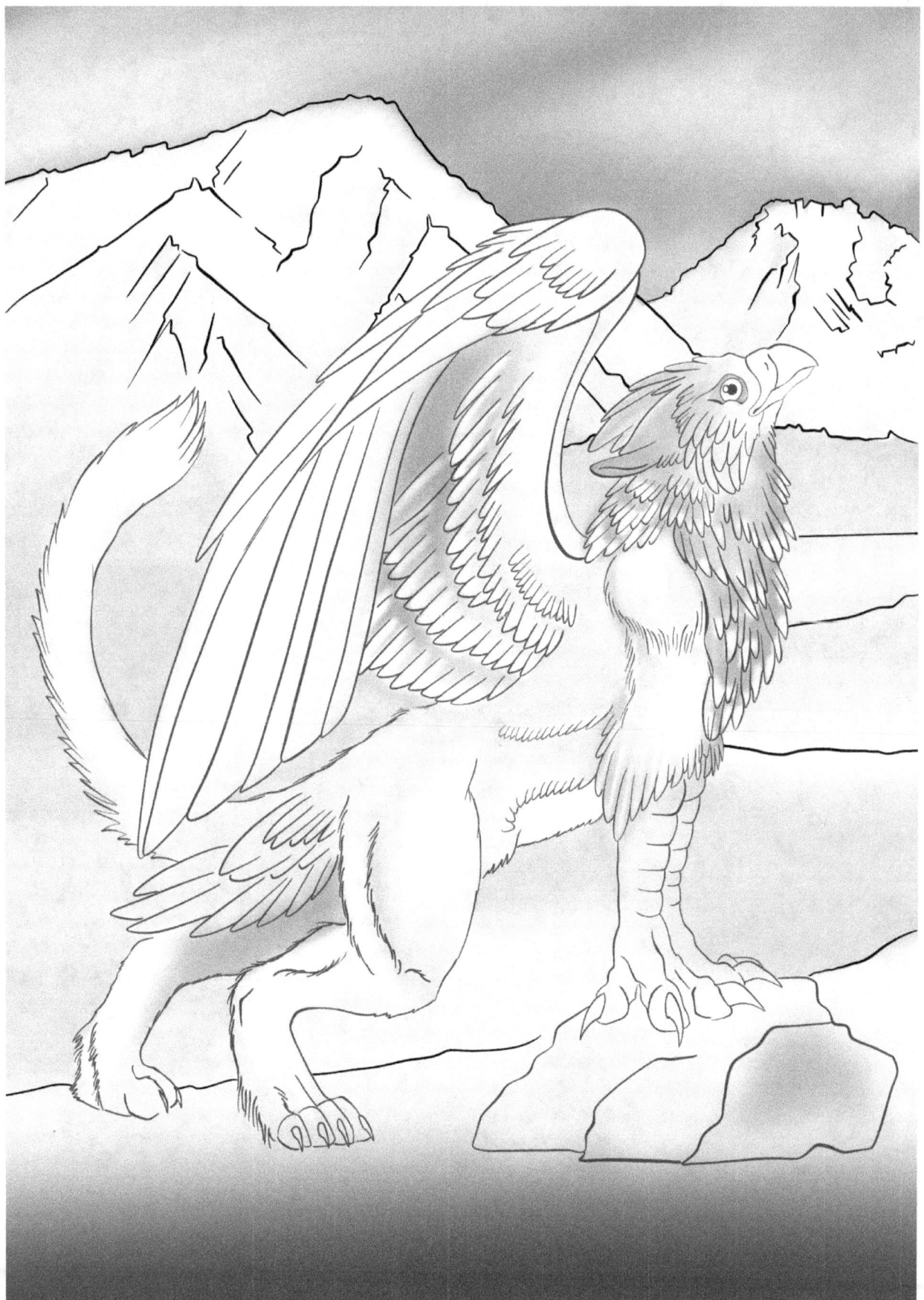

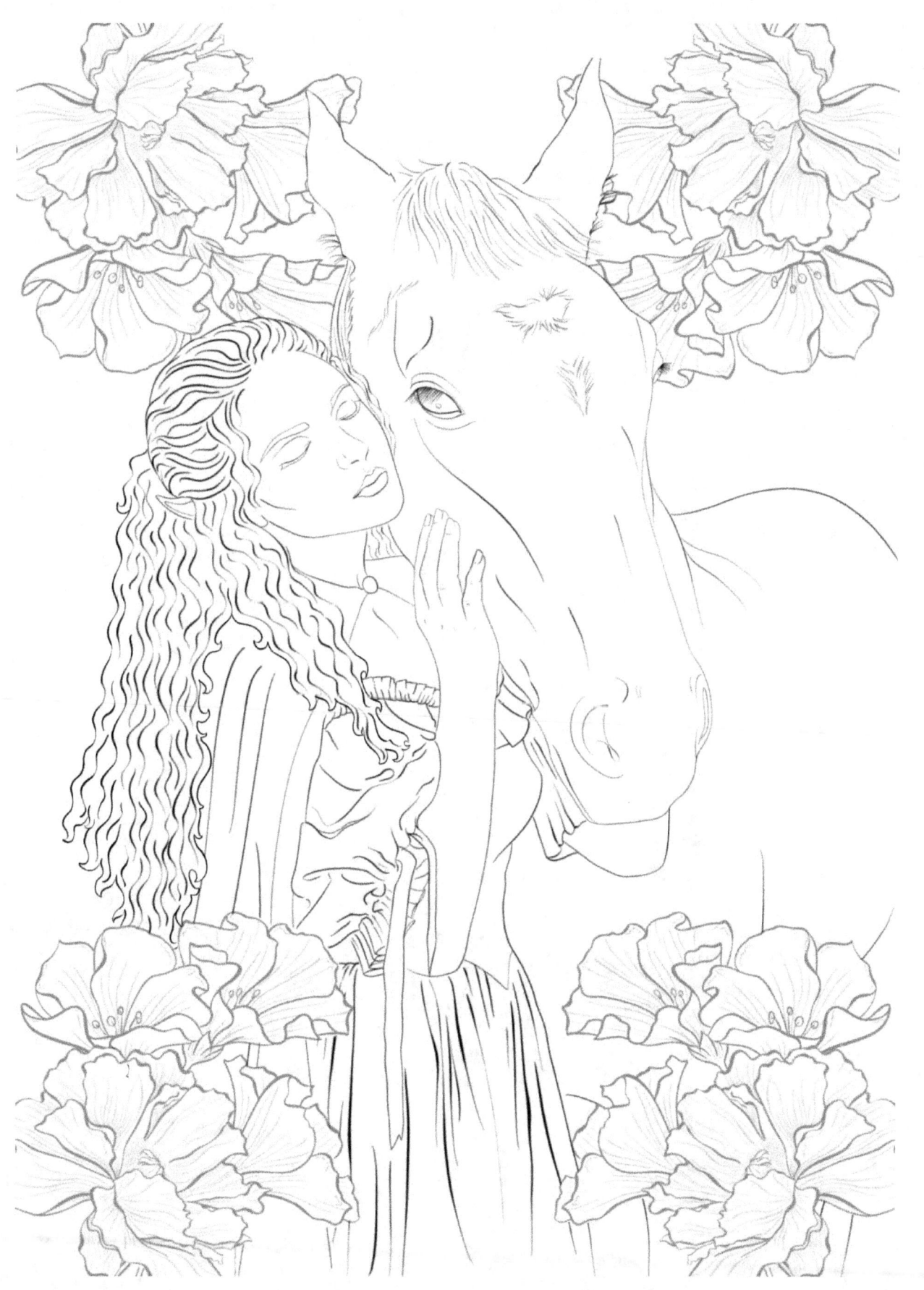

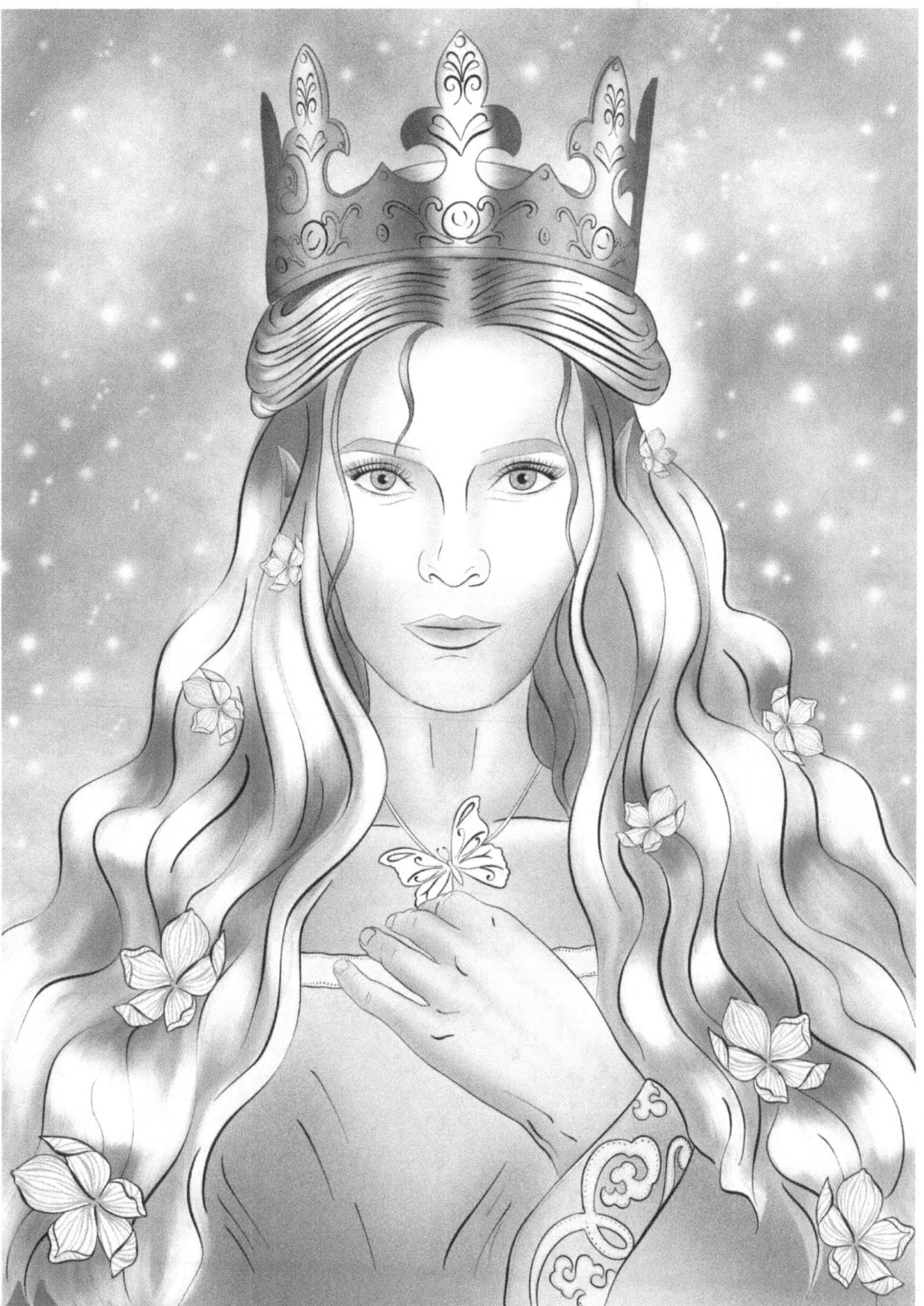

www.ingramcontent.com/pod-product-compliance
Lightning Source LLC
Chambersburg PA
CBHW081747220526
45468CB00008B/2269